George Grube

A PROFESSOR IN POLITICS

Jennifer Grube Podlecki

Prominence Publishing. www.prominencepublishing.com

George Grube: A Professor in Politics/Jennifer Grube Podlecki. -- 1st ed.

ISBN: 978-1-988925-67-7

Contents

Foreword

Although I knew of George Grube beforehand primarily through his book on Euripides, I first met him when I walked into his office at Trinity College, Toronto, in September 1964 to enrol as a graduate student in Classics. It was less than a year after I had arrived in Canada from the UK. George Grube was, at the time, the chairman of the Classics graduate program at the University of Toronto. Learning that I was interested in doing a thesis on Aeschylus, he told me I needed to read all 19 plays of Euripides in the original Greek asap, and offered to meet me, after I read each play, once or twice a fortnight. He need not have offered to do this, but it was the first of several acts of kindness on his part.

He often gave me off-prints of his recent articles and once presented me with a copy of his paperback Aristotle on Poetry and Style (1958) which I still possess and is still in print over sixty years later. Grube was at the time working seriously on a book: The Greek and Roman Critics, published in 1965 for which he won the American Philological Association's award for "outstanding contribution to classical scholarship". When Professor Grube was tutoring me, I did not have a large, financial scholarship and, at one point, I found myself flat broke. I went and told him. "We can't have that," he said. Then, pointing to a pile of 160-180 undergraduate essays on Greek tragedy sitting on his desk, he added, "Why don't you mark these for me?" I do not remember how much I got paid but, whatever it was, it saved me at the time from the anxiety of possible starvation.

There was another side to G.M.A. Grube's public life of which I was completely ignorant, but which, had I known about it, would have been a great boon to me in understanding this strange new country in which I found myself. I had been a student activist as an undergraduate in the UK, with rather eccentric, left wing views. In my naivety, I thought students at the University of Toronto were decidedly unpolitical and showed little interest in political debate. It was a time of affluence with a Conservative Government at Queen's Park; if ever the term socialism cropped up in the media, it usually seemed like a dirty word, evoking images of Reds under the bed. The Cold War was still at its height.

Yet, here I was, having a weekly tutorial in 1964-65 on Euripides, completely oblivious that I was sitting on the other side of the desk from one of the preeminent Canadian socialist intellectuals of the time – one who had had taunts with racist overtones hurled at him in the Ontario legislature (Grube was Belgian by birth) and demands at an earlier time that he be dismissed from his teaching post. The general view was that "professors should stay out of politics". Sir Edward Wentworth, the first Canadian President of the Canadian Pacific Railway, even once magisterially proclaimed that "Socialism was surely an inappropriate doctrine for a university professor to embrace".

Not a word of George Grube's political beliefs ever passed his lips during my tutorials with him – so much for him crossing the bounds of academic propriety by proselytizing his socialist views. Yet, as I think back, there was perhaps one thing that might have given me pause for thought. "One summer, several years ago," he once said, "I decided to read in Greek all the surviving plays of Euripides. The result was my book The Drama of Euripides" (1941).

Euripides was the most controversial playwright of his age. In his tragedies he was never afraid to treat themes that might cause him to be the subject of opprobrium or ridicule among his fellow Athenians. In 415 BCE, for instance, shortly before the Athenians embarked on their largest and, as it turned out, most foolhardy military venture, Euripides produced his famous tragedy, Trojan Women, which even now is often regarded as the greatest anti-war play ever written. Later, towards the end of his life, Euripides left his beloved Athens, as it seems, in despair and died in exile.

As a callow youth who served as a translator in WWI between the Belgian and British armies, George must have witnessed at first hand many of the atrocities of that horrific war. As a result, at the end of the war he, not unreasonably, felt an attraction for pacifism. Whenever I think of the criminal loss of human life in that same war, the words of Wilfred Owen always echo in my own mind, "What passing-bells for those who die as cattle? / only the monstrous anger of the guns..." As the debate raged about Canada's involvement in WW II, when war was declared in 1939, what opprobrium did George's unpopular, political views incur from his fellow citizens? Did he empathize with Euripides' isolation and did he turn to him for comfort as so many of us classicists have turned to our own favorite ancient authors in times of crisis? Was this the origin of his 1941 book?

Although George Grube never professed to be primarily a student of Greek philosophy, there can be no doubt that the thinker who most engaged him was Plato. He once told me that he spent a whole night, before taking one of his finals at Cambridge, reading Plato's Symposium in Greek. Plato was the subject of Grube's first book Plato's Thought (1935), still a concise and worthy introduction to that most elusive and subtle of Greek thinkers. Such is the brilliant artistry of Plato's style that sometimes I just look at his prose for the joy of it. After his retirement George Grube translated and published several of Plato's dialogues right up until shortly before he died in 1982. These translations, including Euthyphro, Apology, Crito, Meno, and Phaedo, were designed to be of scholarly service for students without a knowledge of Greek and are still in print. Also, still in print is Grube's translations of The Meditations of Marcus Aurelius, done earlier in 1963. He clearly saw the need that, with the increasing popularity of courses of Classics in translation, and with the growth of Political Science and Philosophy students lacking a knowledge of Greek, there was a demand for serviceable texts of important classical authors in English. That so many of his translations are still in demand forty years after his death is testimony to Grube's prescience and skill as a translator.

Also, among the works of Plato that George Grube translated was The Republic (1974) which was updated by C.D. Reeves in 1992 and is still available. To my knowledge Grube's translation is the only one done by a Canadian into English. The central issue for discussion in The Republic is how can an ideal society be created based on justice. Pierre Elliott Trudeau drew on this famous dialogue for his campaign slogan "The Just Society" in the 1968 election campaign.

All his life Georges Maximilien Antoine Grube sought ways to understand and make Canada a fairer and more just society, whether as the President of the Toronto branch of The League For Social Reconstruction (LSR), as the editor of Canadian Forum (1937-41), or as the President of the Ontario Executive of the Co-operative Commonwealth Federation (CCF), the forerunner of the New Democratic Party (NDP). At the founding convention of the NDP itself at Ottawa in 1962 Grube was one of the co-chairs. Without the support of the NDP, Lester Pearson's minority Liberal Government may not have succeeded in having passed in the House of Commons in 1966 the Canadian Universal Medicare Act. George may not have been on the deck as one of the commanding officers of the NDP's ship at the time, like Tommy Douglas and David Lewis, but we can be sure he was helping provide the ballast that ensured its smooth sailing.

It was serendipity that brought me into George Grube's office in 1964. I owe the goddess Fortuna a great vote of gratitude. I can only hope that Jenny Podlecki's biography of her father gives him the recognition, at long last, he richly deserves.

Josh Beer

Founder and co-Chair of the Ottawa Society for the Arts and Sciences

Chapter 1: Beginnings in Belgium (1899-1914)

Although my father, George Grube, was one of the leading Classical scholars of his generation, he was the only professor I know of to lead a double life, devoting equal energy to academic and political pursuits. His successes at the ballot box may not have equaled his international reputation as a Classicist, but he was one of the early socialist back room boys who devoted their lives to laying the foundation of the Co-operative Commonwealth Federation (CCF) and who made possible the successes in the early 1990s of the New Democratic Party (NDP).

Georges Maximilien Antoine Grube was born on August 2, 1899, in the northern seaport of Belgium, Antwerp. His parents, Antoine and Marie, were not religious; in fact, he followed them in remaining an agnostic throughout his life. Family legend says that his Flemish nursemaid whisked him away as an infant and had him secretly baptized a Catholic.

Changing one's country, as he was later to do, was not new to the Grube family, for his father had been born in Holland and returned there to live for ten years before coming back to Belgium. His mother's maiden name was Reiners and there were German and Scandinavian strains in her background. My father had the startlingly clear blue eyes of the Dutch, and a straight northern European nose. There is a photograph of him and his sister Lucie when they were very young -- she must be about 3 and he under a year -- which my cousin in Brussels had enlarged. Their strong characters seem to shine forth in their eyes.

Life's experiences did not dim their strength. In their Antwerp home the Grubes spoke French, the language of the educated middle and upper classes up to the middle of the 20th century. They also knew Flemish as it was the language spoken to shopkeepers and other tradespeople. Georges' mother was a woman ahead of her time. She not only was educated but also worked as a teacher and school principal in the first public school for girls in Antwerp. His sister, Lucie, three years older than he was, became an accomplished careerwoman too, director of the local YWCA in Antwerp. She believed in women taking their career responsibilities seriously. My cousin Hari surmised that theirs was not a happy childhood. If they did not finish a meal their father insisted that they finish it before they could begin the next.

Georges and Lucie became orphans at an early age. Their mother died in 1910 when they were 11 and 14 years old and their father died the following year. The children went to live with their maiden aunts -- Augusta, Julia and Berthe -- who were very poor but very kind. There was little money to raise 2 children. When his only pair of shoes needed mending, Georges could not attend school. Missing school was a real deprivation, for he liked it, and did well. School was preferable to staying in the cramped quarters of the attic garret he shared with Lucie. He never forgot the generosity of the aunts in taking them in. The letters he wrote when he lived in England as a schoolboy, as legible as if they were written yesterday,(1) are affectionate and open. As a youngster in Belgium, he was outgoing

---

1. The letters to Belgium may be read in the archives of Trinity College, the University of Toronto.

enough, the family story goes, to be the life of the party at New Year's.

In 1910 Antwerp was still a walled Northern European medieval city. It retained much that was out of place in the twentieth century. Most people lived within the walls of the city unless they had a country estate. Like a village, the town of 300,000 was cosily situated in the shadow of the cathedral, whose tower symbolized the uniqueness of the city. The church owned the cathedral, but the whole city owned its tower, and the people felt it belonged to them.

Sundays were a delight. Georges loved to spend them walking in his city. He would start in the morning from the area in front of the central station and make his way to the boulevard. He passed hundreds of old houses, the living reminders of the town's long history from Roman times. The old imposing medieval castle -- the Steen -- stood at the water's edge as a municipal museum. Within a stone's throw was the old House of the Butcher's Guild, its outer walls ten feet thick or more, meant to withstand a siege. There was a wall around the whole city, but there were gaps: the bourgeoisie did not feel the need to make it altogether impervious to an attack. Generally, people preferred to live within the walled city, so the buildings reached up to the sky. Georges was glad he lived within the walls; it gave the city a neighbourly feeling. Antwerp was the home of the famous Flemish school of painters in the 17th century, Rubens, van Dyck and the rest, and he could stop in at any of Antwerp's galleries and view their works -- landscapes and portraits that seemed to express the eternal truths -- or admire the artists' statues in the public squares. He spent most of the day walking up and down Antwerp's main boulevard, where the people of the city and the neighbouring towns liked to greet each other. Even though the tables at the cafés clustered deeply upon very wide sidewalks, he knew where to find his relatives and friends, the cafés where they would be talking politics. He liked Antwerp best in summer when the boulevard was like an open-air club. If one had visitors from outside, the first thing one did was to take them to the boulevard for a pastry and coffee to introduce them to the ambience of the city. If he himself had been away for the day on a Sunday excursion to Bruges or Ghent, he just had to walk out of the station in the evening and he would find a friend.

Sundays were special as all week his relatives worked hard, very proud of their reputations for not loafing. They told visitors that in Antwerp people walked quickly from one place to the next, whereas in Brussels (twenty-four miles away) people strolled about. They looked on Brussels as a flighty, luxurious place where no real work was done, "a place without any shape to it, with no real history behind it like Antwerp or Ghent or Bruges."(2) On Sundays, Georges loved the music that one could discover everywhere in the city. All the musicians from the towns around came to the city for the holiday. If the players were good, they might get a bandstand engagement or gatecrash the parks that were reserved for concerts. Georges found those concerts "very beautiful."(3) Often the orphan boy gazed proudly upon the tower from his attic window and felt the historic spirit of his city. The tower looked with pride on Antwerp as a splendid trading centre, the Venice of the 16th century. It had seen the horrors of the Spanish Inquisition. Under its shadow the people of Antwerp had fought for independence from the Spanish, the French, the Dutch and the Germans. During each siege and battle, its people felt deep anxiety for the tower's safety.

Georges was already taking a keen interest in political matters. Though young, he took the side of the less privileged Flemish in

---

2. "My Home Town," a series of radio talks on scenes of childhood "Far Away and Long Ago," Friday, June 16, 1939. (Toronto to National Network p. 5 of script)
3. Ibid., p. 6.

political discussions in Antwerp. Even then it was obvious he was not going to be one to sit back and watch what he felt were injustices take place.

In 1914, the war broke upon this charming city, as it did upon hundreds of other cities, with a sudden brutality. Georges' relatives had never been interested in being soldiers. They, and their Flemish neighbours even more so, looked with interest toward Germany for its seriousness, discipline and education. Gifted students he knew were more likely to head for Germany than for the Sorbonne. As recently as 1910, Germany had taken the place of France as Belgium's main trading partner. Everyone knew the military officers were the only people to admire France more than Germany, in order to classify themselves higher than the country-bumpkin Flemish boys who served under them. These officers warned of the seriousness of the danger of a German attack. Most people Georges knew thought neutrality was a real possibility and the best road to follow. At the time when the Belgians finally got around to mobilising their troops, a strategy in case of German invasion had still not been determined.

On the eve of Sunday, August 2, 1914, Georges's 15th birthday, the German minister handed the Belgian Foreign Minister a demand that the German army march into Belgium on the pretext that the French were coming through Belgium. One hour later the Belgian cabinet dared to refuse entry to their giant neighbour. Georges and his relatives had never felt so fiercely proud of their native land. On August 3, the German minister was told of the Belgian refusal. The next day, the Germans invaded, while all the Belgian political parties put aside their differences to applaud loudly the thrilling speech of their King Albert in Parliament. In the cafés, normally buzzing with political discussions, Georges heard none of the usual disagreements about politics. People were unanimously against the German invasion.

From the beginning of August until the end of September the tension mounted in the walled city. Georges and his aunts heard the noise of the guns coming closer and closer. They felt mounting fear as the nearby villagers crowded into the walled city for protection. The Germans were about to put the city under siege. The refugees from the villages had to escape to Holland before the siege began. The orphan children, Georges and Lucie, must go as well. The Germans had spread horrible rumours about the behaviour of the Belgian soldiers towards Germans, with gross stories about atrocious tortures. The Germans had given themselves an excuse to make severe reprisals. The aunts feared so much for the children in their care, especially Georges. He had been already directing traffic for the resistance along with his Boy Scout contingent. Aunt Berthe did wish he were less aggressive and outspoken. She was determined that the children escape. Horrible stories of how the Germans were ravaging Belgium were spreading through the city. Belgian youth must escape. The bombing had already begun. The two orphans hurriedly packed their few possessions in one suitcase.

Georges felt fear for his aunts in leaving them. He hated leaving the dear cathedral tower of his native city. He hurriedly said goodbye to a few of his friends and assured them he would be back very soon. He had got somewhat used to the loss of his parents, but the thought of fleeing his city -- the city which he felt belonged to him -- caused a new kind of pain. It was October 8, 1914, the night before Antwerp surrendered. Georges and Lucie took their one suitcase between them. Lucie kept bossing Georges about what he should take. They were among the 1,400,000 -- one-fifth of the Belgian population -- who left their country. The two teenagers hurried along, sick at heart about leaving their aunts. Several miles out on the road to Holland, they looked back to see Antwerp in flames in thirteen different places. At the docks, the petroleum reservoirs were belching out huge flames into the sky. The whole town seemed to be burning down. Above it all, in dark and silent relief, the tower of Antwerp's 15th century cathedral reached up to heaven, standing as it had stood for centuries. Georges determined to return as soon as possible.

Hearing more about German atrocities even as they fled, the two teenagers alternately ran and trudged their way through Holland and escaped by boat to England. It would have been interesting to read the diary they kept at that time, but unfortunately it has been lost. In the nineteen-eighties, when she was also in her own eighties, Aunt Lucie was asking if I knew where it was. Two people who had shared so much in their early years were close in a way that distance or years or lack of letter-writing could not change. They understood each other; they got annoyed at each other the way only close siblings can. My father always spoke of his sister as fat, though I never thought she was. He used to say she could never have had her illustrious career for over fifty years if she had not lived within walking distance of her work. My aunt felt that she, Lucie, was the one who understood her brother's Belgian side best and that Georges' wife was too Anglo-Saxon to understand him. Lucie complained how he was spoilt as a boy and allowed to escape chores, for he was the scholar, and couldn't be disturbed when he was studying. When she became a widow, she wanted to see him as much as she could. In her eighties, when travel must have been a little uncomfortable and my father himself was not travelling anywhere, she made several trips to Toronto to see him in his Rosedale apartment. They looked alike and, even though living so far apart for over sixty years, their gestures and expressions were strikingly similar.

Chapter 2:
Years in England (1914-1928)

Once in England, Georges, in the thick of things even on his arrival, was busy translating for the English immigration officials on the dock. Dame Elizabeth Cadbury, a Quaker from a distinguished family of Birmingham Quakers, noticed Georges while she was volunteering to help the Belgian refugees. She commented to her Quaker cousin, Ethel Barrow, how good his English was and how she should see that he got a good education. Dame Elizabeth knew Ethel liked children, and her husband Harrison was always busy with city council meetings and his various other civic and humanitarian concerns such as shortening the work week and improving the Birmingham transit system. The warm-hearted Ethel would be a good sponsor, and they could certainly afford it with their chain of Barrow stores doing so well. Harrison and Ethel previously had sponsored refugee children from South Africa whose performance at school had been disappointing, but this boy was obviously intelligent.

Ethel observed Georges as he was translating. Maybe Elizabeth was right: she should try to do something for this clever lad. If he was sent to a home without the opportunities that she could offer him, he might get lost in the class system. The more she watched him the more interested she became in him. He seemed to be in command of the situation. She was sure her husband Harrison would welcome the opportunity to help a Belgian boy. He had been very concerned about the German advance into Belgium. Then Ethel noticed the young boy had an older sister, a stocky girl who was helping the customs officials organize the refugees. In fact, she seemed to be organizing the customs people themselves. Surely a girl with such presence should have the best chance she, Ethel, could manage for her. "Yes, of course," she found herself saying with certainty to her cousin, Elizabeth, "We'll have the carriage bring both the boy and his sister back with us."

As they made their way back to Birmingham, Georges thought that Ethel was the kindest woman he had ever met. She had a certain twinkle in her eye. He didn't know that this was because she hadn't told her husband yet of her plan. When they got to Birmingham, they stopped first at the Cadburys' house. The children felt they were in a fairy tale. The servants were lined up to be introduced to Georges and Lucie. The maids in their starched uniforms curtsied and the male servants in their dark and white uniforms bowed. No one had ever curtsied or bowed to Georges before. He tried to nod his head with the dignity of one accustomed to such treatment. Feeling very lucky, he couldn't help but think of the other students who'd come on the boat with him and he hoped with all his heart that they were as fortunate. They would soon be returning to Belgium, he was sure, and they would be able to swap stories about their English experiences. He'd have quite a story to tell. He certainly hoped some of the doctors and lawyers who had been with him on the boat had not found themselves with simple English farm folk. He looked forward to seeing the refugees he'd escaped with again.

How lucky Georges felt that Ethel Barrow had taken him with her. Georges and Lucie felt welcome in the large and attractive house that Ethel and Harrison Barrow lived in with several servants. The owners, however, did not just sit back and enjoy its luxury. They were fully engaged in the activities of their city and their country. Harrison Barrow was out most evenings at meetings. Ethel went to help in the Adult Education Centre for the workers at the Cadbury factory where each worker was allowed one day a week of classes at the school that Elizabeth Cadbury had set up.

It was a very English household. The Barrows were of stern, hardy stock, originating in Lancaster. The house of Harrison's grandfather George at 1 Hillside St., Lancaster, was and remains a simple cottage near Lancaster Castle and certainly not as prosperous as the one Harrison had built in Birmingham. George Barrow had many children in this small old cottage; his grandson, Harrison, sponsored four refugee children in his large beautiful house. When the Barrow brothers came to Birmingham, two of them married into the Cadbury chocolate manufacturing family, and the two families were very close. Harrison had two brothers and a sister. The oldest, Louis, was a successful lawyer who had four children. His brother, Richard, directed the Barrows' family store, originally an elegant tea and coffee store.

Harrison Barrow became the managing director of Barrows Stores, Corporation Street. Improving conditions in the city was part of his family heritage. His father had become Mayor of Birmingham in 1888. Like him, Harrison worked hard to shorten the working hours of store assistants and for about twelve years he was president of the Birmingham and District Early Closing Association. He was a City Councillor for Birmingham for close to fifty years, first as a Liberal in 1898 and later from 1917 with Labour. On the occasion of his getting the Freedom of the City (April, 1949) he said, "The Council think that, if they have a multitude of Councillors, or by adding to them, they will get more wise. I hope they will." He was elected chairman of the Municipal Bank Committee, chairman of the Traffic Control Committee, and a Governor of King Edward School, which Georges was later to attend. Harrison Barrow was very respected and his knitted brows on a dour face were familiar in his city, but a closer look revealed a bright twinkle in his steel blue eyes.

As a patron, Harrison Barrow was on the stern side, yet he was warm and generous in his actions towards people in general. Because he had done so much philanthropic work for Belgian refugees and for the wives and widows of English servicemen, the British offered Harrison the Order of the British Empire, an honour he had to turn down. As he was on trial for stating pacifist views in a pamphlet, he could not have accepted the OBE. Harrison was one of three Quakers who had published a controversial pamphlet, "A Challenge to Militarism," without first submitting it to censorship. Tried and found guilty, he spent 6 months in a grim jail, where the guards were apologetic and polite to the Quaker gentleman in their care. Since he was rather a fastidious man, the sort who carefully put a newspaper in the basket when he had finished reading it, the experience of being in jail was particularly disagreeable, but he bore it with Stoic resolution.

It was Harrison's idea that during the school term Georges live with a schoolmaster's family, the Richardsons. Mr. Richardson was one of the teachers at King Edward's Grammar School for Boys and was glad to have the extra money that a student boarder from a wealthy patron would bring. Georges was thankful he ate his lunch away from the Richardson home. He could lunch free any time he wanted in Barrows' Stores' fashionable dining room. Like most fifteen-year-olds, he was too shy to dine alone at a table formally laid with white tablecloth and on occasion would prefer to have chocolates for lunch. He wrote to his aunts of his loneliness in

Birmingham, how he missed his relatives and how undemonstrative the English, particularly the Richardson family, were. On the other hand, he found that Ethel Barrow was delighted when, on his way home from school on his bicycle, he stopped in unexpectedly for tea. She seemed to cheer up and become more lively when she saw him. He felt she had a special place in her heart for him, as a natural mother might have for a son.

By March 30, 1915 Georges had learned how to ride a bicycle. He wrote to his aunt that tentatively he might try swimming next. He boasted of winning a water-drinking contest. He now had two pairs of long trousers and wrote that his aunts would find him completely changed. He boasted to his aunt of winning a fight in the school yard despite his "douce et pacifique" nature. He seemed proud of the two black eyes he had for three days as he claimed his opponent had learned not to insult a Belgian. One day, Harrison decided he would help Georges learn how to swim. With his usual determination, Harrison took him out a fair distance from the shore, told him to jump into the water, and then, taking the boat back, left Georges to flail his way back to shore. This was most unsuccessful, and Georges retained a dislike of the water all his life. Harrison taught him to drive in the same manner he taught him to swim. He showed Georges the controls and drove him to the centre of Birmingham whose traffic pattern deserves its name, "The Bull Ring." He got out of the car and, taking a taxi, told Georges to drive home. Somehow, Georges managed to do so. There were no driving laws in those days, so there was no possibility anyone would have to pay a ticket. Perhaps if there had been that possibility, Quaker discipline might have given in to Quaker practicality. The result of his lesson was that Georges disliked driving all his life.

Despite Harrison's strict approach, Georges never doubted his luck in landing on the Barrow doorstep. He put his affection for them in a letter to his aunt in 1917:

Il faut avouer que M. et Mme Barrow sont tout de même bien bon. Ils veulent toujours faire tout pour nous, et cela près de deux ans comme au premier jour. Si tous les Anglais étaient pareils. [Mr. and Mrs. Barrow are very good. They want to do everything for us. Two years later it is just as if it were the first day. If only all the English were like that.]

The school Georges attended was a very good Grammar School. Georges amazed his schoolmasters by winning the only English prize for the whole school at the end of his first term. What a coup to arrive from Belgium as a refugee and surpass the English students in the study of their own literature. The Headmaster emphasized at the awards ceremony at Christmas that Georges had beaten the other students at their own language after only three months in the school. Georges also carried away prizes in gymnastics, geometry, mathematics, the prize for the top marks in his class, and a scholarship for being one of the best students in the school. In Georges' letter to his aunt he wrote: "J'étais fier que j'ai fait honneur de ma patrie." He was proud to have won distinction for his country. He felt that his small country would have need of him after the war. Young men like himself who had been educated in England could make a big difference in the rebuilding of Belgium:

C'est mon devoir envers ma patrie et que je ne serais pas un vrai Belge si j'agissais autrement. Ma patrie, notre cher petit pays, aura besoin de moi et de jeunes hommes intelligents et éduqués comme moi après la guerre. [It is my duty to my country and I would not be a true Belgian if I acted otherwise. My country, our dear small country, will have need of me and other young, intelligent and educated men like me after the War.]

At the same time, as a homesick school boy of 15, he wrote that he was thinking of quitting school and returning to Belgium. Part of the reason for Georges' restlessness was the Richardsons' chaotic home and their undisciplined and noisy children. It was from this experience that he acquired a preference for peace and order in his own family home.

Another thing Georges disliked about the Richardson home was the English breakfasts. He considered these unpleasant and fattening. They consisted of ten ounces of porridge, a few ounces of meat and three ounces of bread and jam. "Not enough bread," he complained in his letter to his aunt Berthe. Mr. Richardson put the scales on the table and measured out the seven ounces of bread a day, a fair amount by English but not by Continental standards. If Georges bought a morsel of chocolate, his landlord said he was aiding the Germans. In a letter written in March 1915, he hoped fervently that the Russians would be in Berlin in two months, so that he could return to Belgium.

He found the Richardson house intolerably sloppy. Mr. Richardson shaved in three minutes, his wife got dressed in five, Mary, the older daughter, got fatter and fatter, Kathleen, the next eldest, more and more capricious. Christine, the youngest, was doing multiplication tables, the dog was being a pest, the cat was flying around eating, and the fourteen-year-old servant girl really appeared to be twelve. He wrote that he regarded all this with a cynical eye and a smile. At night, he would read late into the small hours of the morning, putting a blanket over his door to conceal the reading light. He drew a detailed picture for his aunt of how he would arrange the blanket and stuff the door cracks with clothes and his towel. The habit of late-night reading remained with him for the rest of his life.

Georges continued to be successful at school, despite the chaotic domestic arrangement. For the school English prize, he analyzed Shakespeare's *King Richard* plays and was still able to quote from these verbatim many years later. He became interested in debating and boasted to his aunt that he could speak without notes and won over the native English speakers who brought copious notes to the debating platform. His case was to defend foreign travel by stressing the benefits of seeing different ways of living rather than always staying in one's own country and looking at things in the same way. If you stay a fairly long time in each place and pick up the language and see the habits and customs of the people and then go somewhere else, you have benefitted the most. He also spoke frankly during the debate of homesickness as something he knew quite a bit about. His sincerity put him miles ahead of the other speakers in the eyes of the judges. The only school subject that seemed to disagree with him was Religious Knowledge. True to the humanistic tradition of his family, he found the study of the Bible was giving him indigestion. Two or three times a week he saw his sister after school, and, typical of a boy of fifteen, wrote his aunt that it was often enough to argue with her and to wish not to see her any more often. Lucie was also bright but not so interested in studying as her brother, yet she easily passed her entrance exams to Royal Hollaway College London in January 1916.

Georges complained to his aunt that he had no girl friends. He did meet one Belgian girl in London, but assured his aunt that he had behaved very correctly. He liked the English girls, but not as much as the Belgians, he told her. The Richardsons did make some effort on his behalf. When he told Mrs. Richardson that he never got the opportunity to meet any girls, she arranged a tea party. Young Georges was very embarrassed when he entered the room and saw twenty-five girls of various shapes and ranging in age from ten to sixteen. His landlady in her one effort on his behalf managed to humiliate him. He wrote to his aunt that he had found the whole experience overwhelming.

When one of his aunts came for a visit to London without coming to see him in Birmingham, he was heartbroken and wrote her a poem rebuking her to the tune of the French popular song "Ma femme s'est envolée avec le patissier. [My wife has run away with the pastry cook.]" He planned to go to bed early and dream of finding himself back in Belgium among his relatives. After three years at the Richardsons' house, he wrote of them: "Ils étaient très gentils mais froids et taciturnes. [They were very nice, but cold and taciturn.]" By April 1918, Harrison had arranged for "Tante Julia" Berthe's sister, to be brought to Birmingham for the remainder of the war. Some days Georges would go and walk with her for a mile and a half around the town. Her health was not good, and remained that way until her death on Nov. 8 , 1934. Georges had to take up the English habit at that time of a cold bath every morning when he visited the Barrow home during the school holidays. He did not dare refuse. The funniest thing, he wrote Berthe, is that he had begun to like it. Only when visiting the Barrows at the age of thirty-five would he have the nerve to refuse to start the day in this rigorous fashion. In March 1917, at the age of seventeen, he began to smoke, hiding it from his landlord. This habit remained with him for life. At that time, smoking was considered more a moral sin than a physical risk. At seventeen, he played soccer but called it a sport of brutes and preferred cricket. After college days, he never played any sport, though he did always walk wherever possible. The last sport he played was to be tennis as a student at Cambridge. Smoking had taken over as a habit and he had no intention of giving it up for the occasional opportunity to play a sport.

As a Grammar School student, he spent his four-week summer vacation on a farm at Harrington in North Hamptonshire, where he had promised an old lady he would do her gardening. "C'est la guerre," he wrote resignedly. He would study in the morning and garden in the afternoon. He wrote his aunt that his main friends were the Roman writers Tibullus and Cicero, and the Greek philosopher Plato, as their only faults during their whole lives was to write works that were overly reasonable and rather pedantic. Harrison Barrow insisted he do this gardening job during the vacation with the result that gardening was never to be a hobby with Georges. Many years later, a neighbour on Toronto Island would ask politely if he could come over and take out a few weeds.

What better setting could there have been to further Georges' interest in politics than the Barrow home, where he spent quite a bit of time, thanks to the British system of a month's vacation at Christmas and a month at Easter as well as the summer. Harrison Barrow stood up with courage for his views. Twice his Quaker stand of pacifism interrupted his city council work. It was during the Boer War that he first proclaimed his pacifism. In 1914, Harrison was named Lord Mayor-elect of Birmingham. What a crown for his achievements this appointment would have been. His wife was very pleased at the prospect and even had a beautiful silver pendant made up for herself as Lady Mayoress. But Harrison's pacifism again made him wonder if he could accept the honour. How could he officiate at war ceremonies? How would he perform military duties? Finally, he refused the office of Mayor, but he kept working hard for the betterment of his city on the city council and in other executive positions. As a result of his distribution of a pacifist pamphlet, Harrison had spent 6 months in prison in 1918. Perhaps it was Georges' inability to emulate such a principled life as a youth that turned his energy to scholarship. By 1918, Georges was finding more and more inspiration in the Classics. He wrote to his aunt in March of 1918 that Ancient Philosophy, which was to become his specialty, "est si moderne malgré tout le temps qui s'est écoulé" [is so up-to-date in spite of all the time that has elapsed]." At the same time he worried that perhaps he was neglecting the three-fold division of self that the ancients said one must keep in balance: the physical, the spiritual and the mental, and the balance that keeps the three in harmony. He worried that he might soon become a thinking machine. He was very glad to be able to spend time at the Barrows and wrote of the affection he had for Ethel: "Elle est toujours pour tous d'une telle gentillesse." [She is sweet to everyone.]

The house where Harrison and Ethel lived in Birmingham, 40 Weoly Park Road, in the Selly Oak area, was bright, majestic, and cheerful. Why did Harrison and Ethel not adopt their young wards? Corban Barrow, Harrison's nephew, who was a lawyer with the firm of Louis Barrow (Harrison's brother) and who later became Lord Mayor of Birmingham, said that would have been impossible. Adoption laws came into being in England a few years later, in 1921 when Georges was an adult. My mother confided to me that it would have been better if they had. The Barrows were to leave him more than money as their legacy. The tough moral fiber of that generation of Quakers who were willing to suffer physical hardship for their beliefs was hard to match. Harrison went to jail for his pacifism, as Quakers had done before him both in England and North America.

In the best tradition of his British heritage, he helped those in other cultures, taking both South African and Belgian refugee children into his home. His concern to better the lives of his workers made him a leader in adult education and in improving working conditions. Appropriately enough, so many years later, in 1949, the city of Birmingham made him a Freeman of the City and bestowed on him the keys of the city. In his acceptance speech, he claimed he had contracted arthritis from the curses of other motorists trying to find their way through. After Harrison's death, the Grubes were pleased to have a parchment memorial plaque of this honour on their wall and would show it proudly as they told Harrison's story to anyone who wished to know it, and many people visiting the Grubes in Toronto were very interested. My sister, who was a Quaker, had the testimony to Harrison hanging in her home on Long Island, New York.

To Georges and Lucie, Harrison and Ethel represented outstanding examples of Quakers who were very demanding of themselves. At times, the two refugee children must have felt daunted by the strict standards of the Barrows. Such outstanding morals, how could they live up to them? Lucie tried to with some of them and Georges with others. Lucie, like the Barrows, never let alcohol into her home. She devoted almost sixty years to a job working for the betterment of youth at the Antwerp YWCA just as Harrison had done for the betterment of his city. In his turn, Georges put great emphasis on scholastic achievement. He filled the role of scholar early in life: Lucie was always the one called upon to run to the store for milk or bread if the servants were on their holiday, for one couldn't disturb her brother when he was studying. Harrison Barrow was delighted by the high scholarly awards Georges continued to achieve, winning a scholarship to Cambridge in 1919. Harrison, strict as he was with the Grube children, could be very generous in his personal life. In his eighties, he welcomed my sister into his house when she became a post-graduate student at Birmingham University. Like Lucie, his ward of over 30 years earlier, my sister wished to show her independence by living in an apartment of her own. Again Harrison was rather perplexed by this determination of a young woman in his care to live on her own, but he went along with it.

Even as Georges was trying the Cambridge entrance exams, he still longed to return to Belgium: "Je ne resterai pas en Angleterre plus longtemps qu'il ne sera absolument nécessaire." [I'll not stay in England longer than absolutely necessary.] In this same letter, he insisted that he was achieving scholastically only as his duty towards his country, for he would not be a true Belgian otherwise. He dreamed of spending his many days of holiday in Antwerp, and assured his aunt Berthe not to have the least doubt that he would return.

What interfered with his dream of returning to Antwerp? At the age of 19, he was inducted into the Belgian branch of the British army. On April 28, 1918, he was declared unfit for cavalry and infantry but fit for all else. He boasted that, like the other Belgian students, he had to begin his service with three months leave so that he was "a soldier on leave without ever having been a soldier." He was to serve a year-and-a-half in all, and was in the Eleventh Company in the camp at Anvoivis, Sarthe, France. Most of his company were Belgian students studying in England like himself. How he hated digging ditches in the France of World War I. After the armistice, he served as an interpreter to the British forces in Belgium, and then for a short time with the Belgian army in Germany. In 1918 his letters to his Aunt Berthe go to Hastings, England. Harrison Barrow had already brought her and another aunt, Mathilde, safely out of Belgium. In that same year, when George was on leave from his army posting in France, he promised to visit his sister in London. Lucie had been waiting and waiting for him. He had promised to spend Christmas with her, but where was he? The stories from France were terrible. Perhaps he had suffered from the gruesome gas warfare she had heard was rampant in his part of France. Finally, on the stroke of midnight of Christmas Eve, there he was at the door in his uniform.

He hated army life. Always one to go to bed late, he loathed getting up at 6 a.m. The four hours of exercising every morning and afternoon were excruciating. The food was good but there was not enough of it, and the 3.35 francs a week wage was not enough to live on. With great relief and anticipation, he returned to England to go to Cambridge in October, 1919. He was looking forward to his years as a student at Cambridge. They were going to be wonderful after army life. He couldn't wait to be reading as many books as he could in the Classics again. He'd only been able to take a few with him and he'd read those over and over. He was ready to be inspired by the beautiful sorroundings of Cambridge. The young student could not believe his eyes as he hurried through the lovely gardens of the Cambridge colleges that first autumn of his university career in 1919. The contrast to the horrors of southern France during the war made it seem like the Elysian Fields. His very favourite garden was that of Clare College; he always managed to walk through it when he could. It was smaller than that of its neighbour King's College and reminded him of the gardens of the estates in Antwerp. He liked to go to concerts at King's College Chapel. Although not religious, he loved the music that the College chapels offered. He liked to pause before the splendid statue of Henry VIII over the gate of St. John's College. Enjoying the sense of history that permeated the whole town, he often walked from one part of Cambridge to the other.

England was pulsating with the certainty that the First World War, "The Great War," had been the war to end all wars. There was a renaissance of free thought in no place more evident than England's great University of Cambridge. Socialism was one of the ways the intellectuals were going to herald in a new era. Cambridge students, the cream of Britain's youth, had a responsibility as the intellectually elite to lead the country into that new era. The conservative ideas of the Victorian era must change. Freedom was going to touch all areas of life. Bertrand Russell in 1918 wrote: "Marriage should be a free, spontaneous meeting of mutual instinct, filled with happiness not unmixed with a feeling of awe." (*Roads to Freedom*, George Allen and Unwin Ltd. London, 1918) Education was going to change so that children "may be encouraged to think and feel for themselves, not to acquiesce passively in the thoughts and feelings of others." (Bertrand Russell, *Political Ideals,* George Allen and Unwin Ltd. London, 1917) Progressive schools were putting into practice the revolutionary ideas of the British educator A.S. Neil. Children instead of being seen and not heard as previously were to be given the freedom to learn to read only when they were ready.

Just as Georges was influenced by Harrison politically, so he was influenced academically by his tutor at Emmanuel College Cambridge, the Australian L. H. G. Greenwood. From him he got the idea that in scholarship the important thing was to be as clear as possible in order to be read and understood by as many people as possible. To go off on an esoteric tangent was really a waste of time. Georges and Greenwood corresponded for many years, not only about scholarly matters but about politics. Perhaps they shared being outside the English class system by birth.

Georges, still spelling his name in the French way, worked hard for his three years at University but what a pleasure his courses were. He was required to read the whole of Classical Thought in three years to be prepared to be tested on the complete body of Greek and Latin Literature, History and Philosophy at the end of his third year. There was no question of his or any of his fellow students working at a job during the vacations. They had to spend all their time reading and studying if they were to get through the massive amount of preparation expected of them. Of course, he had to maintain the ever-popular student pretence of not appearing to be working as hard as he was. He had to be seen strolling off to tennis or to punting leisurely on the river Cam in the afternoons. With Georges that was easy as he worked best when everyone else was in bed anyway.

He did like to go with his friend "Luke" (N. B. C. Lucas, later Principal of Midhurst Grammar School and author of *An Experience of Teaching*, Weidenfeld and Nicholson, London, 1975) walking in Wales and on the Continent during "the vacs"-- Luke also had no family to return home to -- but they spent a great deal of vacation time studying as well as walking. At his college Emmanuel, he was able to get closer to his tutor Greenwood than he had to Harrison. Like many Australians, Greenwood was a congenial man. Georges was determined to achieve a First Class degree on graduating from Cambridge in 1922. He wanted to show Harrison what he could do. And he wanted to pay his own private tribute to his schoolteacher mother who had died a decade earlier.

Lucie wanted to show her worth in a different way. At eighteen, she was determined to have her own apartment in London, paid for with her own money. Much to Harrison's distress, she got a job with British Intelligence. Her pacifist patron was very upset. Luckily, Lucie and Harrison were able to talk matters over so she could at least attempt to explain to him why she had to be independent financially. Lucie's great forte throughout her life was that she was able to get into serious discussions with anyone: with her children, or with the young people at the YWCA in Antwerp (and even later, on the plane from Vancouver to Toronto at the age of 80). During the Second World War she was even able to talk to a German SS officer who took her into his office because she went out every evening to the Y to meet her young people. Her husband, Odon Demeure, was very distressed when she told him the Nazis were following her. When one SS officer did take her to his office for interrogation, she said to him, "You believe in youth, don't you? The Nazi youth, and so on. Well, so do I. These young people need me, especially in time of war, so I must go and meet them and talk to them." He was apparently a family man with pictures of his children on his desk. She had no trouble convincing him of her sincerity.

Georges and Harrison could not talk together as easily as Lucie and Harrison. They could both be reserved and stubborn. When Harrison, at the age of 79 was visiting our family at Ward's Island, Toronto, we were all watching a boat on the horizon while seated on the verandah one Sunday afternoon. For the whole time Georges and Harrison argued about whether it was a sailboat or not. Harrison's actual influence on Georges, however, was very great. Like Harrison, he stood up for his principles even though that might mean going against popular opinion. He followed Harrison also, not only in being a political man, but also in being dedicated to socialism. At Cambridge an enthusiasm for debating polished Georges' speaking style which improved with each debate, and he began to feel the power of his ability to sway his audience. He enjoyed playing tennis, punting on the river, and going on walking tours during the vacation. Years later, he would boast that he was the same weight he had been as an undergraduate without taking any regular physical exercise.

It was in his final term at Cambridge, in the spring of 1922, that he forgot his Greek text and asked the pretty girl beside him whether he could look on at hers. Three weeks later, during examination week, they became engaged. Her name was Gwenyth Macintosh and she had also come to Cambridge on a scholarship from a grammar school which was in the fashionable area of Highgate, London. Her family was not rich; her mother had been left a widow with five children when Gwenyth, the youngest, was only two years old. Even so there were servants in the house. When young, she had to eat her pudding before her meat so she wouldn't need much first course, as meat and fresh vegetables were expensive. Her mother felt she was unable to manage five children financially, and so she sent the oldest son, Stuart, to America at the age of seventeen to work in an orange grove.

There were a host of reasons why my grandmother, Annie Macintosh, disapproved of Gwenyth's engagement to George. First, Gwenyth and George had not been properly introduced. It was unthinkable from Annie's point of view that they should speak to each other much less become engaged under such circumstances.

To have attended the same classes for three years did not count the way being formally introduced would. The man Gwenyth wanted to marry was a foreigner. And a refugee at that. In addition, George was agnostic and Annie was devoutly Anglican. To top it all, he was a socialist and Annie was a conservative. Could it have been that Gwenyth, the baby of the family, was trying deliberately to shock her mother? Gwenyth had deeply resented the fact that her mother had followed her to Cambridge to live when she went there as an undergraduate. From Annie's point of view, however, she was just moving back to where her own family, the Greys, had lived and her husband's family, the Macintoshes, had established successful businesses since 1750.

Other people make Annie Macintosh sound much more interesting than Gwenyth represented her. At 19, Gwenyth had been looking forward to being independent from her mother. She knew Cambridge was her mother's favourite place in the whole world and that she, as a widow, deserved to be close to her childhood friends and relatives. Gwenyth really wished she could be kinder to her, but the more her mother doted on her, the only girl of her 5 children, the more resentful she became. Gwenyth's cousin Cristabell, who was two years ahead of her at Girton College, wrote of looking forward to a picnic of young people that her aunt Annie was arranging, as she always gave a good party. Annie, a spirited woman, went to the States to give lectures to various Women's Institutes. One of her motives was to see her oldest son, Stuart, who had never wanted to return to England even for a visit. As Gwenyth had been the first in her family to go to university, she received a great deal of teasing from her three older brothers for being a bluestocking. She never forgave the brother closest to her in age, Felix.

When she was at Cambridge University from 1919 to 1922, the professors often ignored the women in the class, addressing their students as "Gentlemen." The way she chose to react to such treatment was to wear a 'bob,' the short male haircut popular in the '20s, and to smoke a pipe during reading week. During the spring break of 1922, she joined George on a walking trip on the Continent with his friend Luke. Marion Bilson, a friend of Gwenyth's who came along, was very much in love with Luke, but he didn't find her attractive at all. When they arrived at one farm and asked to stay for a small sum, the farmer's wife was delighted and promised them her best meal. She made a large fluffy omelette for starters. The group's eyes widened as she produced another large omelette for the main course and later, beaming, she brought out a third full of jam for dessert.

When Gwenyth became engaged to George, she had already accepted a scholarship to Bryn Mawr College in Philadelphia for a year, an adventurous choice for a woman from England in the 1920s. She didn't want to leave her fiancé but she just could not turn down such a prestigious college as Bryn Mawr. During her year there, she met Helen Young who became a lifelong friend. Many years later, my mother went for one week annually each February to visit Helen: her week off from the family. Sometimes they went to Ms. Young's cottage in Provincetown, Rhode Island. While at Bryn Mawr in the spring break of 1923, Gwenyth, Helen Young and some other college girls took a car to Florida. Although Gwenyth didn't drive, she enjoyed the trip with the other bright young women as they all set out with their hair freshly bobbed and their nineteen-twenties garb.

On her return to England and for a year before her marriage, Gwenyth taught at Bedales, a progressive school in Hampshire. The school received its inspiration from A. S. Neil, the progressive educator whose teachings have been so popular in North America. It was a school founded on socialist principles, but owing to the lack of an endowment and the expense of experimental education, it took in mostly the children of well-to-do parents. As a country boarding school, it was isolated from the rest of national life. The atmosphere was that of a university rather than a school. It wanted to give students the ability to make decisions for themselves, and taught that such freedom of expression involved responsibilty to members of one's community. The only rule the school had was that the pupils had to get up early and have a cold shower.

The greater the effort my conservative grandmother made to influence the engagement of her daughter, the more ultra-modern for the time were Gwenyth's reactions. George, however, got on better and better with his future mother-in-law. George and Gwenyth rather than get married in a church, married at a registry office with only their two fellow students, Marion Bilson and "Luke" present as witnesses. Gwenyth wore a sensible-looking brown suit and cloche-style hat. When the Macintoshes gave them a gift certificate to a very Victorian furniture store, Gwenyth and George refused it as they wanted modern furniture. Annie Macintosh continued to hope to influence her youngest child and in 1935 on the occasion of my birth she sent an expensive white shawl for my baptism, but Gwenyth not only did not have me baptized but had the shawl dyed brown to go with her evening dress. My parents' refusal to buckle to convention continued at my own wedding; when the rest of the wedding party was wearing formal wear, George refused to wear tails, choosing a dark navy suit instead.

On the other hand, Gwenyth took an instant liking to Harrison and Ethel Barrow. She enjoyed the relationship with Harrison very much and was very fond of him. Also she had great respect for the Barrows' Quaker ways and for their politics, which were socialist like her own. The Quaker duty of visiting those in jail and of working on behalf of prisoners was a practice taken up by both George and

Gwenyth. George felt compelled at his first university posting at Swansea in his 20s to teach prisoners in the Swansea jail as a volunteer. My mother played an active role during her fifties on the board of the Elizabeth Fry Society of Toronto.

On graduating from Cambridge, George tried schoolmastering. As Assistant Master at Sutton Valence School, Kent, England in 1922-23, and as a Classical Fifth-Form Master at Highgate School, London, he found that school teaching did not suit him at all. In Kent, as a French teacher, he began instructing the boys by telling them they could do what they liked as long as they told him first in French what they were going to do. Several told him they were going to leap over the desk and promptly did so. Later George would tell the story, pleased that he managed to tell the headmaster he was quitting before the headmaster told him he was fired. His own experiences as a teenager had not prepared him for schoolmastering. In addition, he had little patience and lacked a general liking for children.

The two Classicists, George and Gwenyth, since their first names began with 'G' as did George's last name, Grube, had the old Greek letter digamma engraved on their wedding rings, though the young couple was so poor that Gwenyth's soon turned green. My mother received a great deal of inspiration from her Classical scholarship. Though she was not to continue her study of the Classics -- few women continued their formal education in those days --, she was able to come up with appropriate Classical quotations all her life and much impressed many a gathering of scholars. University lecturing was much more to George's taste, enabling him to pursue his own scholarship and interests. Despite his excellent First Class degree from Cambridge, George did not have the connections necessary to get a university post. He had to apply to several universities until he found his first job as a lecturer. In 1923 he was hired by University College, Swansea, Wales. My father and mother found this setting very provincial indeed compared to Cambridge, but George, as usual, threw himself into his activities. He became sponsor of the Debating Club and was very popular. When he applied for a job at Trinity College, Toronto, S.K. Johnson, the Professor of Classics at Swansea, in his letter of recommendation emphasized how much the students liked George. The Debating Club students presented George with an engraved gold cigarette case dated May 1928.

Unlike other professors from England who had gone to lecture in Welsh universities, he took up the linguistic challenge of learning Welsh. He continued the Barrows' interest in adult education. One of his cherished memories was a talk on Athenian democracy which he gave by candlelight in an attic to a group of Welsh miners. He told the graduating class of 1962 at the University of Toronto that he was thrilled by the experience and so were the miners. Unable to buy a car due to his low salary, he bought a motorcycle much to Gwenyth's concern and made several weekend trips to London for culture. The Grubes bought a modest house, which they owned for many years as they decided to rent it after they left rather than take a loss on a sale.

On May 11, 1927, George and Gwenyth had their first child. They named her Antonia Joan, Antonia for the heroine of Willa Cather's *My Antonia* and Joan after George Bernard Shaw's *Saint Joan.* That they chose literary heroines for their first child shows how true and important the ideas of literature were to them. One of the literary heroines, Antonia, was from the New World, suggesting that North America may have had an appeal to them even then.

The Classics professorship at Swansea came vacant. There was only one professor in each subject in those days at British universities. George was a candidate, but the post was awarded to a much less qualified individual. Having been dealt with unfairly made the young couple less contented with their lot. Gwenyth felt very isolated being at home alone with a young child after the exciting life she had had as a student at Cambridge and Bryn Mawr, and as a teacher at Bedales. She had never had to do housework or cooking as her mother always had servants. George felt he could not visit his relatives in Belgium even if he could afford it, as he would be drafted again. On July 12, 1924, and again on January 28, 1925, a letter from Belgium came to Swansea saying he was in no way released from military service now he was a British subject, and he must attend the annual review of soldiers 'en congé' [on leave]. He closed firmly the Belgian chapter of his life, and became more and more British in his ways. With enthusiasm, he became involved in University activities.

Just as George appeared to be settling into university life in Swansea, he quarrelled with one of the university administrators in the Common Room on the subject of politics. Expressing sympathy for the Welsh miners, he contradicted the political opinion of an important university official. This was quite typical of George who was never one to hide his political opinions, no matter whom he was addressing.

Their stay at Swansea was to last four years. After a probationary term as Assistant Lecturer from 1923-26, he was appointed immediately to a full lectureship. Already active in several university committees, he served on the board of the Faculty of Arts for three years and was a member of the University Senate and a member of the student committee. He was treasurer of the Students' Union Council. He was on the central executive of the University Teachers of England and Wales. During the absence of the Head of the Classics Department for a term, he conducted his work. All this before George had reached the age of twenty-nine.

In the spring of 1928, he applied for the Classics professorship at Trinity College, University of Toronto. His Cambridge tutor, L. H. G. Greenwood, wrote a letter of recommendation. George had written long letters to his tutor after graduation. Greenwood claimed he was "eminently a man who can think for himself in matters of scholarship and who has energy and initiative in the practical things of life." Greenwood continues, "He has very markedly the gift of speech and is likely to be successful with large and popular audiences." In light of George's many speeches later both on the political and academic platform, Greenwood's analysis was certainly correct. His only weakness, according to his old tutor, was he had never studied Classical verse composition, that is, he had never written poetry in Latin and Greek.

The other person to write a glowing recommendation was the professor at Swansea, S. K. Johnson. He had, in fact, got the job George had put in for and was probably uncomfortable having his more well qualified competitor around. In his letter Johnson spoke of George as a first class man, a very promising scholar with a particularly attractive personality and a strong, virile manner. He continued that he was unusually popular with students, and capable of dealing with large "unruly mobs" as well as select honours students. George had contributed very conspicuously to the administrative work of the department. Johnson called him idealistic, with the ability to communicate those ideals to others. Johnson thought George's knowledge of French might be of value for a Canadian university professor of Classics as Canada was a bilingual country. Another correspondent to the Provost of Trinity, Prof. Conway from England, mentioned George's eagerness to come. A letter of recommendation from Emrys Evans, Principal of University College of Bangor and former Professor of Classics at University College Swansea, told of George's vigour, his practical initiative, and that he had been responsible for the establishment and success of the college Classical Society.

Provost Francis Cosgrave, the head of Trinity College Toronto since 1926, was going to have Gerald Larkin, who was on the board of the college, interview George when he was visiting his relative P.C. Larkin, the High Commissioner for Canada in London, but he later decided an interview was unnecessary. The credentials were impeccable. The job was offered for $3,700 per annum, to be paid in twelve installments. There was an allowance of thirty-five English pounds for expenses for the journey from Swansea to Toronto.

Chapter 3: Beginning in Canada (1928-1934)

To start fresh in the New World, the land of opportunity, seemed a good idea to George and Gwenyth. In late spring 1928, George accepted the professorship at Trinity College, Toronto. The only way Canada could get qualified people to come from England at that time was to offer them full professorships. Trinity also promised him that, if everything worked out all right, he would become Head of Department after a couple of years. The officials who made this arrangement did not inform the rest of the Trinity College Classics department about the promise of the headship. Naturally, they were taken by surprise when George assumed administrative authority over them in September, 1931. It says something about the restraint and courteousness of both sides in those days that they could live with a situation that remained ambiguous for some time. George had to remind Provost Cosgrave of his promise. As the Provost wrote in a letter dated May 25, 1932, he had forgotten that he had made George Acting Head and not Head the previous autumn.

There was a very close relationship between the Grubes and their new boss. Many years later, when George was in his 70s, he was to refer to Cosgrave as "a great personality... he gave a sort of tone to the College." (Robin Harris' interview p. 23) Since the Grubes' first accommodation in Toronto was not going to be available for the beginning of the academic year, the Provost offered them rooms in his own house until they could move. This generosity was particularly welcome as the Grubes arrived hot and tired after their train trip from Montreal with their year-old daughter. The Provost was under the burden of being their host while his wife was on a visit to Ireland. George was later to show the same hospitality to a new member of his department, Alex Dalzell, and his wife in 1954. The Grubes offered them their Toronto Island home until they found a place of their own.

The early days in Toronto were not an easy adjustment for the Grubes. The house they had rented at 24 Howland Avenue was grim, gray and Victorian. For one thing, they had very little money. As a professor at a private college, he earned 10% less than he would have at a public institution such as University College. Long afterwards when I walked with my mother past the row house where they had first lived in Toronto, I was horrified by its dinginess. In Toronto in the late 1920s and early '30s, the difference from their Cambridge milieu must have been a great shock for my parents, especially for my mother, a bright Cambridge graduate. George for his part had found enough congenial colleagues by 1929 to start a petition protesting the way the police circled a meeting in Queen's Park of a group interested in peace, the Fellowshp of Reconciliation. Because 68 professors put their signatures to the paper within 24 hours, it was called the Letter of the 68 Professors. Professor Meek had insisted he be able to follow his usual route to campus, and a police officer twisted his arm behind his back. Of course, George was one of the first to instigate a protest.

What encouraged George and other similar-minded individuals to adopt a stance of vigilance against such repressive tactics was the extreme Protestantism, with its narrow thinking, which had such a stranglehold on the city. Even much later when I was only in grade 5, we were asked to stand up as good examples if we had been to church on Sunday. I made an arrangement with a friend's family to go to church with them, as that seemed to be a prerequisite for attending school without the risk of being shamed. The great excitement of the year was the Orange Day Parade, a virulent anti-Catholic demonstration -- to which I persuaded my mother she must take me.

In the early days my mother did some teaching at Trinity College. There is a letter in the Trinity archives dated 1930-31 from the Provost to my mother thanking her for the two hours a week of teaching at $250 for the year which she had done to fill in after the sudden departure of a professor for Jerusalem. But life in Toronto must have been intolerable for the bright young woman who had rebelled against her family's conservative traditionalism. The fact of graduating from Cambridge put her on a level apart from other women in Toronto at that time. She kept telling them a degree from Cambridge was not all that impressive, but they didn't believe her. She was very isolated, and not used to managing a house without servants to help her. She returned to England.

From 1932 to 1934, my mother taught at the innovative school Dartington Hall in Petersfield, Hampshire, and this was very much to her liking. The school was a reaction against the strictness of Victorianism. It had been financed originally by Dorothy Whitney Straight, who came from a wealthy U.S. family and was the wife of the U.S. diplomat Willard Straight. She had put up the money for the Joas ballet when it was driven out of Germany. There was an aura of chic and flair about the school: Bertrand Russell's son, Viscount Amberley, went there. At the same time it included the village children. As a bright young woman graduate of Cambridge and Bryn

Mawr, Gwenyth found the place very congenial. She invited her students to supper Wednesday nights. When a female student told my mother she would like to have her Greek tutorial on the roof, and then turned up in the nude, my mother had the sang-froid to continue the class as if nothing were amiss. As it was a bitter day with the wind howling, the girl never tried the experiment again, although she did last for the full 50 minutes of the Latin class. The girl had been expelled from 7 Convent schools and had a certain determination.

On my mother's return to Canada in 1934, the Provost again offered her temporary teaching. More important to her, she joined The International League for Peace and Freedom. She became friends with enlightened women such as Mary Sissons, wife of the University of Toronto historian, C. B. Sissons, and Alice Loeb, the socialist wife of a well-off cement maker. Trinity College didn't have a Wives' Club, although Victoria and University College did, and I doubt she would have joined in any case. It would not have suited her as an intellectual to be in a women's club whose only common theme was where their husbands worked. She would have been included in a certain number of college functions, as "Trinity was a very friendly place." (Robin Harris' interview with George p. 32) George recognized that the ease of lifestyle Trinity offered its professors was supposed to make up for a reduced salary. As he said to the Executive of the college: "We enjoy the amenities of Trinity and our wives pay for it [with their small amount of housekeeping money] at home."

Women my mother knew tended to get involved politically because of local issues which affected their families. Margaret Mackenzie, wife of the later University of British Columbia president Norman Mackenzie, got Mary Richardson, lecturer at the University of Toronto, to run for the Board of Education because the washrooms at their children's school, Brown Public School, were so terrible. There was no thought of pay for members of the Board at that time. Some of Gwenyth's women friends of that era were to last a lifetime, such as Nellie Fraser, who was a kind of aunt to me. She was a widow who had been left with three children to raise on her own. Later, since she lived opposite my high school, I used to have lunch with her occasionally. Only those friends of the same political persuasion as herself did Gwenyth tolerate. George's view of human nature was not so politically exclusive. Although emotionally involved in politics, he did not, for example, change his doctor when the family doctor, Jacob Markowitz, stopped supporting the CCF.

In the period 1929-33, George had not yet found the best outlet for the political interest he had acquired from Harrison Barrow and indeed from the Classics, that a man has a duty to his city and country. George followed the Greek belief that to be apolitical was, according to the ancient Greek source, to be an *idiotes*, from which, as George and Gwenyth both liked to point out, we get the word 'idiot.' Prof. Sissons took George along to a political meeting of the Co-operative Commonwealth Federation, and the interesting calibre of the people involved immediately impressed him. Sissons was the kind of man George felt a sympathy with: he was a Canadian, a progressive, and a radical. A Classics professor and scholar of some note, he was also a historian. Fascinated by the Canadian experience, he wrote a book on Edgerton Ryerson and was committed to combating anti-French sentiment in anglophone Canadian intellectual circles. In other words, he was just the sort of man that George would like.

As time went on, the CCF made possible my parents' adjustment to Canada. Before they became dedicated to the CCF, they had been looking eastwards to England for their inspiration. After both their experiences of the 1920s at Cambridge and my mother's at Bedales and Dartington, they had felt constrained by the atmosphere, the prejudice, the blue laws that were Toronto in the 1920s, 1930s and later. In 1936, eight years after their immigration to Canada, George applied for the only job he was ever to apply for after he had got the appointment at Trinity. In order to be near the Barrows, George applied for the chair of Classics at Birmingham University. Gilbert Norwood, his very dear friend and colleague at University College, Toronto, wrote in his letter of recommendation that George was the most accomplished Classical scholar of his years in Canada. The letter continued, his "administrative ability shows energy, common sense, tact and patience." By that time, he had been for two years chairman of the four colleges' Classics departments, and Secretary of the Graduate Studies Committee. But there was still energy left for more. He still felt unfulfilled. George and Gwenyth needed a spiritual commitment.

That they found in the CCF. The Co-operative Commonwealth Federation, the socialist movement originating in western Canada, held its founding convention in 1933 in Regina, Saskatchewan. George joined the CCF in 1934, and his dedication was to last until his death in 1982. My parents enjoyed the contact with Canadians from every walk of life. Their friends in politics became our family relatives. The devotion showed to some of these people by my parents and their responding affection could not have been closer if we had been related by blood. Our home often had out-of-town socialist visitors staying overnight or coming for a meal. The CCF was our extended family. Frederick Philip Grove, the Canadian writer, stayed at our home when he was a delegate to a CCF convention. He loomed tall and one had the impression he had to stoop to fit into our small East End home. I remember a return Sunday visit of our family to his large red brick old Ontario home in the country. The land was scrubby and I had my first impression of an artist's poverty.

His wife, dressed in black, showed the facial anxiety lines of a difficult life.

Just as we had overnight visitors, so George had his favourite CCF hospitality stops. One of these was Walter and Marjorie Mann's home in Ottawa. When I talked to her about it much later, in 1988, Marjorie still remembered the first time George came, when Walter called up the stairs to ask if it was all right if George Grube stayed overnight and she replied loudly and reluctantly, "I suppose so," not realizing that George was standing at the bottom of the stairs. He wrote her such an elegant bread-and-butter letter afterwards that they became friends for life. Walter said George lent an old-world Continental charm to the CCF. Eugene Forsey, later a Liberal senator, who stayed frequently in 1943 or so when he was a CCFer, was my favorite "Uncle" and I thought he was very handsome. In the National Archives there is a letter Forsey wrote to Frank Underhill in which he criticizes George for taking on so many tasks and thereby earning both his admiration and despair.

George's political experience of working with outspoken critics in the CCF must have been useful in dealing with academics, who can be less direct than politicians in their criticism. He himself used to say as Head of a department that he was very good at appearing to run a democratic Classics department by consulting his colleagues before a decision was made, though one gathers it was usually his point of view that won out.

From 1933 to 1935, George was a founding member and president of the Toronto branch of the League for Social Reconstruction, a lively group of left-wing thinkers. In 1936, he was also its acting secretary. Toronto in the early thirties had more to offer an intellectual man than an intellectual woman. George had already changed his country twice and was ready to devote his energies to his academic job and his political life. As president of the

League for Social Reconstruction, he made himself and the secretary ex-officio members of all LSR study groups. He wished the groups were willing to call in experts to address them, but they preferred to thrash out the topics themselves. The Canadian historian Kenneth McNaught remembers that as a boy he could hear the exciting, animated discussions when the LSR met in the living room of his parents, the Carleton McNaughts.

George was very concerned about the subject of pacifism and offered to prepare a paper on the topic. He considered himself a pacifist, but not with the firm basis of the total commitment Harrison Barrow had. A person had to think realistically. What could one do to prevent war? What would one do if war came, and what if one were asked to take part? One hundred and twenty people attended the January, 1935 gathering. He held the executive meetings in the large home at 44 Farnham Avenue that he and Gwenyth had rented for $60.00 a month on her return from England in 1934. The garden party he held in June of that year for the whole LSR was a big success. He felt it important to have 2 to 3 socials a year. Paying for the refreshments was a small price for the feeling of good fellowship. It was an effective way to get new members in. They came to a social, and signed up for a study group. On another occasion George gave a talk on education. Advocating that money be put toward good vocational training, he urged that such opportunities were important for those who could not manage university. He was proud of the university where he taught and felt it maintained a high standard. He was glad to do more than his share of serving on executive committees there. He found himself doing more than most on the LSR and became advisor on publications as well, reviewing all the pamphlets that were recommended by people. But, he thought, if he was doing most of the work, perhaps the group had outrun its usefulness.

As he became more and more involved in the CCF, he grew impatient with the long-winded discourses of his academic colleagues. He began to confide in a few people like Eugene Forsey that he thought the LSR was not getting anywhere. In fact, he recommended it fold. He felt in his heart that political action was the only way to accomplish the goals discussed within the LSR. He was turning more and more to the CCF as the only worthwhile course and others were coming to the same conclusion. The networks and links with the LSR still remained vital within the CCF. Canada's population was small and the fact that someone had been involved wlth the LSR was still important within the socialist cause. Charlie Millard of the Steelworkers Union, for example, hired Margot Thomson because she had connections with the LSR. Other networks were equally important. Margot Thompson had been active in the young peoples' socialist group on the University of Toronto campus, the CCYM (Co-operative Commonwealth Youth Movement) which, besides having political discussions, also did a lot of activities for enjoyment. The trade-union movement itself was in touch enough to be aware of this group, since the student population was small. Because other groups offered political action as well as discussion, the LSR was losing its vitality. Eugene Forsey confided to Frank Underhill (May 4, 1941) on the subject of the LSR: "I am more and morc inclincd to think George's suggestion is the best: dissolve."

George was inclined to withdraw from what he had begun to lose interest in. The LSR had been useful while it lasted; the discussions had been fun as well. On the other hand, he was much more interested in the CCF with its variety of Canadians than in a group mainly limited to academics. The only element he was to miss was the contact with young university students. As he became more and more serious about politics, he had less and less time for talking extra-curricularly with students.

From the early thirties, Trinity College remained a safe home from which he could branch out into other activities. For one thing, it had been in fact his home when his wife went back to England from 1932 to 1934. During this time, he lived in the old Trinity residence at the southwest corner of Harbord and St. George. There were interesting scholars available to converse with. One could always count on C. E. Ashley in Economics or Lyndon Smith in Religious Knowledge. The Shakespeare critic Wilson Knight was an enjoyable character. One evening, about 10:30, when George was passing his open door, Knight called out to him, "Have you heard this?" As George entered, Knight read him the opening lines of *Measure for Measure*. "Listen to this," Knight continued and read out the whole play, acting out all the parts, jumping on the furniture and running about. George knew he was privileged to listen to a genius who loved Shakespeare and he sat spellbound until 2 a.m. Knight directed productions of Shakespeare at Hart House, the student centre at the University of Toronto, and George took part, fascinated to see the Shakespeare scholar at work. He knew he had a good speaking voice. He attended some of the debates of the Trinity Literary Society and he took an active part. He still felt the excitement in the debating process that he had found as a 15-year-old.

Trinity continued to be his home. It was invariably where he took his morning coffee in the Senior Fellows Common Room -- professors were sometimes known as Senior Fellows following the British system -- and there he could count on a diverting game of chess. He often took his lunch and dinner at the Head Table in the old oak dining room of the college with the portraits of former dignitaries regarding him. It was a comfortable life, though he realized his wife was helping to support it because the salary he took home was less than that earned by professors at other colleges, due to these privileges. When others sounded him out about leaving the college to which he had become so accustomed, he had to try to put into words the reasons he did not wish to leave. The family knew it was because he liked his college life and his political life. In December 1947, E. R. Dodds, Regius Professor of Greek at Oxford, wrote to ask if he would be interested in a Readership in Ancient Philosophy. He couldn't offer a professorship as there wasn't one at Oxford in this field at that time. George felt buoyed up enough by Oxford's approach to look at his position in the University of Toronto with new eyes. Surely he did not have to teach so many undergraduate classes that he had to refuse to direct graduate theses with students who requested to work with him. In 1948 he wrote to Prof. Jeanneret, Director of Classics at the University of Toronto, to ask for some relief from teaching. If he could get a grant of $1000 or even $750, he could make better arrangements for the next year. In 1949, the University of California at Berkeley approached him. When George refused, the Berkeley Classicist W. H. Alexander wrote to say that he could understand George’s reasons for staying in Canada. Alexander was sure life in the United States would have been easier than in Canada. George could have worked comfortably at the Classics he knew and loved, and would have escaped his Canadian political responsibilities. Alexander appreciated George's feeling he had to stick it out where he was. To George, it would have meant an evasion of his duty.

The next year his old political Tory rival in Broadview, Tommy Church, died. George knew the Broadview CCF people would want him to run again. Before the election was called, he had better get everything straight with the Trinity authorities. First, on February 17, 1950, he requested and got permission from the then Provost, Reginald Seeley. The Provost warned him to keep in mind the regulations of the college. George assured him his election duties would not interfere with his teaching. Defeated roundly, he decided not ro run again. He had to admit to himself he really did not like electioneering. In September 1951 the University offered him the prestigious position of Head of Graduate Studies in Classics, which was a five-year appointment, and he was pleased to accept it as recognition for the work he had done for Classics at the University of Toronto.

One of the remarkable aspects of the Trinity College atmosphere was the gentlemanliness of the combatants when a disagreement was taking place. There was a running battle about politics in the Toronto *Globe & Mail* newspaper between George and a right-wing theologue, Frank Beare. During this fiery exchange, the two political enemies continued to play chess with each other in the Trinity common room quite amiably. Two others of George's chess partners crossed theological lines: Lyndon Smith and Eugene Fairweather. Part of the tolerant atmosphere was due to the leisurely lifestyle at Trinity. It was no disgrace to play chess after lunch until 2 p.m. An hour over a discussion at dinner was normal. Very few people rushed away at 5 p.m. It was a home away from home where married professors frequently stayed for dinner and worked in their offices in the evenings. George often did so, as did Philip Child, the novelist and professor of English.

Another factor that made for tolerance at Trinity was the inclusive nature of the Anglican tradition in colleges. As the Established Church in England, it looked on its theological activity as a process of formation rather than a dogma to which all had to adhere. Anglicans thought it natural to have rationalists on its college's teaching staff. The first colleges formed throughout Canada were Anglican. Bishop John Strachan had started King's College which was the predecessor of Trinity. The rules were much stricter at the nonconformist colleges. At Victoria College, of Presbyterian origin, there was no sherry allowed on the premises until about 25 years ago. In contrast, the Anglican church wanted to have a broad base so as not to alienate its members.

After the 1950 by-election, illness struck the Grube family again (my sister Toni had been seriously ill during her third year at Trinity). This time it was my brother John, who contracted Maria Strumpilitis, an arthritic disease of the lower spine common in young men, and he could barely walk for months. With faltering steps, he made his way around the block every day. The illness had been triggered during a summer job lifting beer cases for a warehouse company. The whole household had to organize itself around the invalid. George felt very guilty about his family responsibilities. Could he have prevented John from catching this crippling disease? Once again, generous friends came to the rescue. Just as during Toni's illness, when a friend had given $100 to be passed on when some other person's family was in need of it, so now the father of one of George's students, a wealthy New York businessman known affectionally in our family as 'Pop Wiegand,' sent money to help with John's "medical, educational, or recreational" expenses.

Berkeley approached George again in 1952. He was tempted. It would mean a release from his executive responsibilities in Toronto both political and academic. They took a great deal of his time and the salary was tempting. He would never have had to be concerned about money again. He still found himself worried about the financing of his children's education. His older daughter, Toni, was about to begin her first job; John had been hit by arthritis, but would certainly qualify for graduate school, and I, the youngest, had university yet ahead of me. The only course was to go to the President of the University of Toronto and explain his dilemma. The President immediately called Provost Seeley at Trinity and said, "Don't let Grube go." An increase in salary was arranged.

Chapter 4: Political Activities (1934 on)

What accounted for 48 years of such committed involvement in a political cause? One factor was the people in the movement. Esther Birney referred to the group that she and her husband, Earl Birney the poet, and the Grubes belonged to as 'bright and sunny.' There were many social occasions, she added, of a casual, almost family nature. I remember at one such Sunday afternoon gathering at the Birneys noting how everybody really liked one another. According to Esther, there was 'a lot of laughter.' Mary Millard, a University of Toronto student in the forties, whose mother Mary Richardson was active in the CCF, recalls there were a lot of social activities such as teas and dinner parties. Toronto had little variety of entertainment and what there was closed down entirely on a Sunday because of the Protestant blue laws. You could be arrested for having a beer in your own back yard on a Sunday. At twelve midnight on a Saturday night, you could not order a drop more liquor in a restaurant. Yet people were ready for a bit of fun on their day off.

Another element that bound the group together was the respect the early socialists, including George, felt for J.S. Woodsworth, the leader of the social democratic movement both inside and outside Parliament. He was not a legend that became greater with time, for his followers' great loyalty to him was there right from the beginning. When Woodsworth died suddenly in 1942, I remember my parents' grief was as great as if a dear relative had been struck down. There was much in the movement that my parents found attractive. Not only were there other diverse and interesting people in the socialist movement such as Earl and Esther Birney, Andrew and Peggy Brewin, Ken and Marion Bryden, but there was an energy generated by the movement itself and by the variety of the different types of people working in it.

The CCF filled the great gap in George's life that had been left first by his departure from his own country as a refugee boy of 15 and later from England, the country that had given him his educational opportunity. Cambridge remained the source of his academic inspiration. He went there almost every summer in the 1930s until the Second World War made visits to England impossible.

George enjoyed public speaking. He had debated and won at school and at Cambridge University. As faculty advisor to students both at Swansea and at Trinity College, he conveyed his enthusiasm for this art to the young. He read widely what the rhetoricians of Greece and Rome wrote on the subject. His ability came into play at political gatherings. The severing of the English connection by the Second World War made him turn with energy to Canadian socialism.

The CCF provided a great escape for the Grubes from the narrow prejudice of parts of Toronto in the 1930s. I remember even 15 years or so later, in 1945, an example of this aspect of Toronto on VE day in my grade five classroom. I have a vivid recollection of an unpleasant incident. The teacher made a Jewish boy stay in for an indignity she had imagined, but we all knew it was really that she didn't like Jews. As the bells of Toronto were peeling out the sounds of victory, we were experiencing in our east Toronto classroom a version of the prejudice which had made Hitler famous. All the children in the classroom were aware, the way children are, of the irony of the situation.

The original inspiration for George's political action was 5th century B.C. Athens, as his popular lectures on Greek democracy showed. The Athenians viewed their politics and their ethics from an aesthetic point of view. To live in harmony, to have the various aspects of one's life in accord with each other, was the ideal to be aimed at. The three aspects of the continuous process that leads to progress roughly corresponded to three kinds of personality: the politician, the educator, and the prophet. The philosopher king had the ability to handle general ideas, the detachment necessary to do so, and the power of clear and concise expression, all in a fairly well integrated personality. Plato in his concept of the philosopher tried to unite all three, although he failed to do so in his own life. One of democracy's greatest problems was to get the three kinds of persons to work together: the practical man, the teacher, and the dreamer. George could not understand and did not admire the complete lack of interest in the science of politics on the part of most of his Canadian colleagues and other intellectuals, and he contrasted it with Britain in the interval after the First World War. He had the following advice for any philosopher who plunged into political life: Go in quietly and unobtrusively and, if you are willing to serve, you will soon find yourself leading due to your command of words. You can never use any word, phrase, or part of a sentence which, taken out of context, can be misrepresented to mean something which you did not say.

Unlike the Spartans who came as conquerors, Athenians believed they were indigenous to the land, and confident enough to offer their city as a refuge to newcomers. Foreign settlers played an active part in Athens' business and intellectual life. They could even become citizens. The city derived strength from its ability to combine local tradition with new blood. The tradition of hospitality was one that George practised in his own life. Whenever a visiting Classicist came to the University of Toronto, it was George who held a party at his home to honour the dignitary. As Head of the Graduate School in Classics from 1951 until his retirement, he invariably entertained at his home at 5 Washington Avenue, and he personally funded many such a festivity. He considered it worth the cost of entertaining to create a warm welcome for the visitor and to give staff and often graduate students in Classics the opportunity to communicate with the visitor on a personal level. He was proud of the fact that the University of Toronto had a very high reputation in Classics. At one time in the 1950s the number of graduate students coming to study exceeded the number of undergraduates. George, sympathetic to the plight of graduate students often far from their homes and without much of a campus centre at that time, always had a welcoming supper at his home for them at the beginning of the academic year.

Free speech was one of the tenets of Greek democracy and it was a right that George practised despite the difficulties he encountered from speaking his mind. The degree of free speech the average Athenian citizen possessed was very great. Even Socrates, according to George, could have avoided the death penalty. Throughout his career George continued to be one of the most outspoken members of his college Common Room, just as he had been -- and had consequently got into trouble -- as a young man in his twenties in Swansea. Part of this was due to the fact that he thought it important that educated persons think clearly and use their own language well. One should have the courage to stand by one's convictions. Educated individuals should be ready to defend the truth as they see it -- an uncomfortable and sometimes dangerous activity. They should also have a sense of history and a social conscience. Other ideals of Greek democracy were devotion to the common good, respect for the law and equality before it, the viewing of wealth only as a means to a common end, intellectual curiosity, full opportunity for discussion and debate, versatility and free choice of jobs -- all of which George considered still to comprise the academic ideal, and values still worth striving for in a modern democratic society.

The Athenians looked on recreation and leisure as basic rights. George told graduating students in a Convocation lecture in 1962 that they must allow themselves time for these two necessities in their lives. Leisure was the time remaining after one had refreshed oneself through recreation. Leisure should be used for creative purposes. Every educated person should have at least one hobby which is culturally, socially, or politically useful. Both leisure and recreation are necessary to make one fit for work again. He confessed to this graduating class that he found timetabling his day just as bothersome a problem as he had forty years earlier as a new graduate. In an entry in his diary when he was 42 he wrote that he was so busy that he felt his leisure time a bit strained, and recalled a man he had taught with in his first job who had said he had no time to be amused, and how ridiculous George had thought him at the time. George also wrote in his diary that he wished he had a competent secretary, for then he should have lots of time. People thought he had so many interests. Perhaps if he were to realize his secret ambition of being a writer, that might bring him the sense of work well done. He would like to write a book on democracy. He jotted down some of the ingredients that might go into such a book. One must have faith in the common man; every man has a soul. He would discuss the limits of the talents expected from the ordinary man in a democracy. Such a man had to be honest and courageous. He had to practise self-control, since the Greeks thought moderation a great virtue. He had his social duty towards the gods of the state, and there was a close connection between the good man and the good citizen.

He thought that in Canada, the machinery necessary to give this capacity full play was two levels of compulsory education, the primary and secondary. The political instrument was the CCF and the economic instrument the Trade Union and the Farmer Associations. Politics should be considered the kingly science, and interest groups must apply pressure to safeguard their concerns. Elections must be real and fair.

The young Athenian interested in democracy made athletics his recreation. The ideal athlete was good at all the sports of the pentathlon: running. jumping, wrestling, and discus- and javelin-throwing. The Olympic victor even received free meals at the public expense, but it was the amateur with all his charm and weaknesses, and with his interesting personality, that was glorified. The amateur must be capable of well-sustained effort; he was in no way a dilettante. George quoted Pericles's Funeral Speech as recorded by the historian Thucydides to illutstrate this point: "We love beauty without extravagance; we love knowledge without being soft."

George looked on himself as an amateur in many ways. He never got a PhD -- it was not necessary for an academic in his day -- and he would have hated to have had to specialize on a remote topic which he felt few would be interested in reading about anyway. He wanted to reach as large an audience as possible with a topic of general interest. Only one book which he had written would have got him a Ph.D., he claimed. All the others, he was sure, would not. He used to say the universities had Ph.D.-itis, that is ,"the ridiculous idea that every university teacher should make an original contribution to knowledge." (Nov. 7, 1973 interview with Robin Harris, p. 9) In his department, he hired 3 Classicists who, like himself, did not have Ph.D's: John Cole, Mary White, and Ron Shepherd. He found Plato inspiring to read, and wanted to convey his enthusiasm to others. He recounted his first reading of Plato's *Symposium*:

> *I began reading it after dinner one day in my rooms about 7:30. I finished at 3:30. I should have been quite incapable of passing any searching examination on the text: I did not even look up all the words, only the essential ones, but it remains an unforgettable experience -- and from that day I should never have dreamt of reading a dialogue in translation.*

Others' interpretations of Plato left him annoyed. In a 1936 review of W. F. R. Hardie's *A Study in Plato*, George caustically warned readers to “be on their guard against the occasional confusion which results from blaming Plato for not taking modern philosophers into account." About H. Gauss's 1937 *Plato's Conception of Philosophy*, George writes cryptically: "I doubt whether much is gained by such exhibition of Plato in modern dress. Would it not be better if, after drawing their inspiration from Plato, modern writers had the courage themselves to wear their own opinions?" He was always concerned that the student of Classics should look at the text itself. In a 1937 review, he remarks, "There is little here which the reader cannot find for himself in the Platonic text, or with the help of the better commentaries."

Plato wrote that a man had a duty to serve the society he lived in. For years, George maintained an unwavering commitment to work on committees both for his university and his political party. The actual length of time he spent on both was phenomenal. One of the University of Toronto archivists said he served a much longer time on committees than most professors. He did not always do exactly what the president of the university wished. When Sydney Smith was trying to make the vote from the university senate unanimous to give Lord Beaverbrook an honorary degree, George and Cecil Lewis, who was professor of German at Trinity, kept voting against it. Many professors told George afterwards they agreed with him but did not dare vote against the president of the university's wishes. According to my mother, when George was in a meeting, he could discern the root of a problem from which a way could be found of finding a remedy. Through his objective viewing even of everyday problems, he could help one find a solution. In a note to himself which is not dated, he writes:

> *It is perhaps natural to get excited where one is oneself involved -- but actually one let oneself be involved where, personally, one actually was not, by identifying oneself with certain group interests such as CCF etc. This was no doubt the source of one's driving power, and it was difficult to preserve one's balance.*

According to his former pupil Margaret Sedgewick Lazaros, he would get so emotionally committed to a point of view that he would storm out of a meeting if his motion didn't pass. At times he could be very objective, but if the matter were important to him, he would show how upset he was if the tide of thinking was against his own. In an address to the Classical Association of Canada, he saw two main responsibilities for Classical scholars: to awaken a widespread interest in the Classics, that is to provide good Classical fodder for the general public; secondly, to train teachers filled with enthusiasm and capable of communicating it.

Although he was certainly very available, my regret is that I didn't bring enough of my problems to him. As my mother said on more than one occasion, he was very good in a crisis. My sister Toni told me that in our family situation, he claimed that he never said the wrong thing, and this was true. When I talked to Esther Birney about my father many years later, she remarked, "He was not a chatterer at all but what he did say was very much to the point." As she put it, "One felt safe with George due to his gift of discernment and objectivity." Interestingly enough, my childhood friend Christina

McCall used this same adjective. When, as an adult, she was the Grubes' neighbour, she said she felt very safe.

On the other hand, he did enjoy a fight for what he thought was right. An encounter that might send others running for cover was to him really worthwhile. Always concerned with the issue at hand rather than with personalities, he could sound infuriatingly rational to his opponents. Such an occasion arose in 1939 just prior to the Second World War when he spoke against a motion at a CCF convention suggesting that the $63,000 the government had voted to help Britain's war effort was excessive; the government should put some of the amount to peaceful purposes, such as looking for a solution to unemployment and improving health care. To those governing Ontario such words smacked of disloyalty and lack of patriotism. The Liberal Premier, Mitch Hepburn, and the Conservative Opposition Leader, Col. George Drew, immediately attacked George and the co-sponsor of the motion, Frank Underhill, a professor of History at University College, Toronto. Drew descended to extraordinary invective, calling George a "foreign rat" "easily discernible by his name," who was "trying to sink the ship of state." The Liberal representative from St. Paul's riding threatened to sever relations between Trinity College and the University of Toronto: "There is no doubt we have the power to do it.... I am a precedent buster, it has been said, and I am prepared to break a precedent now in order to hit at a man of the character of this foreigner Grube." The more Drew and Hepburn and their cohorts ranted and roared the more my father continued to sound rational. This tactic won him wide support across Canada. Even the resolution itself calling for munitions money to be used for work projects represented the opinion of many Canadian people. My father rather enjoyed the whole thing, though my mother was worried about how she would feed her family if he were fired.

Was the uproar justified or was it just a tempest in a teapot? In spite of his tendency to love a good fight, George did admit the uproar was unjustified. In a letter to the Provost of Trinity (April 27, 1939), he wrote: "An unfortunate juxtaposition of words causes offense and rouses bitter and violent criticism where the same position, formulated more carefully, would raise objections but not an emotional storm." In other words, if the resolution that Frank Underhill had drawn up had had less passion and more forethought the debacle would not have ensued.

Since his own college was private and therefore privately endowed and not dependent on the government for money, it could come to George's support and did, as Hepburn and Drew were the kind of political upstarts that Trinity, which was rather traditional, could not abide. The Provost of Trinity at the time, Francis Cosgrave, and a powerful member of the Board of Governors, Gerald Larkin, were 'small l' liberals and didn't care for the kind of right-wing anti-intellectualism that was at the root of the attack on the professors. Frank Underhill's college, University College, was dependent on government funding and could not take the same stance. My mother told me Underhill did not enjoy the fight the way my father did. Underhill had a different temperament, one which might enjoy goading with the tip of his sword rather than going directly into battle itself. He and George had completely different personalities and had led totally different lives. Underhill came to Toronto as a star from a small town in Ontario, and George from his international background. He lost all patience with Underhill and finally managed to get the message through that he wanted no more of his shilly-shallyings. For the next forty years of his life, he managed to keep Underhill out of his path. Since Canada's population, let alone its population of intellectuals, was not large, and, in addition, at one point Frank's wife Ruth was my teacher, this was no mean feat. From Underhill's point of view, George's habit of playing psychologist to his friends must have been exasperating, as this April 25, 1952 letter to Underhill shows:

> *Your best friends, of whom I am one (whether you think so or not) know very well it is high time you did face yourself if you are to do anything more than work off your own frustrations onto other people in print, or have anything like the influence you could have and should have. (Underhill papers. Public Archives of Canada)*

George did not mince words; he said bluntly what he thought. He was a formidable opponent, even for the Premier of the province. When Premier Hepburn called Provost Cosgrave on the phone, the Provost told the Premier of the province with what must have been a mischievous Irish twinkle in his eye that he was sorry but he couldn't recall anyone named Hepburn on the board of governors of his college. He knew he was talking to the Premier of Ontario. Letters of support for the two professors poured into the newspapers from across the country. The newspapers themselves wrote lively editorials in support of freedom of speech for the professors. The expressions of righteous anger poured in from across Canada. An editorial in the Montreal newspaper *Le Devoir* entitled "L'affaire Grube-Underhill" condemned the lack of free speech in Ontario. From the west coast, J. S. Woodsworth wrote congratulating George on his handling of that "Colossus that is Ontario." From Calgary, M. Cartwright wrote, "There is much Hitler-ism in some of our legislators and our democracy needs a great deal of enlightenment" (April 16, 1939). In the spirited style for which he was known, Eugene Forsey wrote of the "vileness" of "this shameful attack." He continued, "Be sure to let me know of anything you think we can do. Otherwise don't answer this. Heaven knows you've enough on your hands." A lively cartoon in the *Winnipeg Free Press* showed the premier and the leader of the opposition proclaiming "Free speech -- but only for us." Its editorial on April 15, 1939, concludes "We cannot afford to turn Nazi to fight Hitler. If we do, we have lost everything worth fighting for even before a war begins. The *London Free Press* claimed that a professor of Classics was being "muzzled" and "discriminated against in a way unworthy of any democracy," and went on to call such an action "regimentation of the true Hitler type." (April 15, 1939) The *Windsor Daily Star* pointed out that if the British Empire stood for anything, it stood for democracy and freedom of speech, and to suppress free speech was merely to copy the tactics of dictators. The *United Church Observer* warned, "The question of the right of men of education and training to speak their minds has been openly challenged." (April 15, 1939) Henry Somerville, editor of *The Catholic Register*, wrote that there was more academic freedom for Prof. Frank Scott in Quebec, that it was less Pickwickian, than in Toronto. In contrast, the *Globe & Mail* editorialized, "Whether or not disloyalty is taught in college classrooms, it is being taught outside, and will make progress only as the teaching of loyalty is neglected in the lower schools... the place where respect for the British flag and love for British institutions" is nurtured. From across the border in Buffalo, an anonymous "Well-wisher" wrote on April 14, 1939, "I wish to compliment you on your courageous utterances recently publicised. Time will prove you right when Hepburn will be forgotten except as a bad dream."

George's old friends in England heard of his fight and sent him letters of support. One from a friend at his old school, King Edward's, Birmingham, begins, "Good cheer! Delighted to see you are still at it," and continues, "I'm surprised at their going for Underhill. Isn't he a Canadian?" One of his former students, Kingsley Field, wrote from Woldingham, Surrey, that he had read in the *Evening Standard* of the Premier's threats and was there anything he could do to be of assistance?

Premier Hepburn and the Conservative opposition leader, George Drew, found themselves punching at shadows. George was charged in the House of Parliament with making "seditious utterances." But an editorial in the *Ottawa Evening Citizen* (April 17, 1939) objected that sedition was a serious accusation and needed defining. It was too elastic a term, according to the editorial, but not elastic enough to embrace the statements complained of. Luckily the then Prime Minister Mackenzie King played the whole matter down: "To take official cognizance or action on every public statement of that nature would place upon the government a heavy and new responsibility." (*Evening Telegram* April 13, 1939)

Hepburn and Drew threatened to bring in legislation to separate Trinity College from the University of Toronto to try to make the college fire George, but Trinity stood behind him. Many sent the Provost personal letters of support for George, like that of Ella Mahony:

> *Further as a Canadian citizen, I should like to join with all lovers of free speech in the hope that the day is not far distant when teachers of Prof. Grube's type will be able to use their exceptional gifts for the benefit of the community without fear of senseless persecution.*

George was to remain loyal to his college for the rest of his life. He wanted his family to be loyal to it, too. When I wished to transfer to another college after my freshman year, he wouldn't let me. Since he was paying the bills, I had to acquiesce to his strong feeling on the matter.

When George first stood for Parliament in 1940, he was invited to dinner by the wealthy and much respected Gerald Larkin, a benefactor of Trinity College, who headed the Salada Tea Company. Larkin said that he thought that it was an excellent idea for university professors to stand for Parliament, as it wasn't common in those days for professors to make such a commitment, especially in view of the salaries they earned and no time off for campaigning. Many people expected them to keep out of politics entirely. George Drew made the statements in the legislature which showed his disrespect for educators. Ironically, he was later made chancellor of an Ontario university.

Chapter 5: Political Activities (1940s)

Having the support of his college and winning national favour in an argument concerning freedom of speech with the leaders of the Ontario legislature was one thing but winning the East End riding of Broadview-Greenwood in Toronto in the 1940s was quite another. Our family moved to the riding which my father was hoping to represent. It was a very mistaken notion, as I could have told him after only a few weeks of playing on the street, that my father of all people could persuade those hard-core conservative, British-stock Canadian working-class people to vote socialist. No one who had been born abroad and had a foreign name could have won their vote. We really were outcasts in that neighbourhood. Being a sociable sort, I played with the children on the block anyway but it was certainly not fun. They were very prejudiced. Since my mother was an intellectual, the women ostracized her. When the soldier next door returned from the War, his wife had everybody on the block to a party to celebrate -- everybody, that is, except us. As for socialism, our neighbours thought it was the work of the devil. At the time of the 1943 election, I was eight years old and happened to be skipping with a group of children on the street when Ken Bryden, the CCF organizer at the time, and Morden Lazaros were canvassing, that is, knocking on doors and talking to people. When they came to the door of my friend's house in front of which we were playing skiprope, the lady at the door could not have been more horrified if a flasher had appeared. She shrieked for her sister to come. I remember how sad I found the whole incident. Of course, the old parties knew how to stir up this fear the ordinary uneducated person had of socialism. The media also could whip it up. The constituency we lived in voted for the popular Conservative candidate Tommy Church again and again.

Though George ran in three federal elections in 1940, 1943 and 1945, and one by-election in 1950, he was defeated each time. His most successful run was in 1949 when he came within 1000 votes of Tommy Church. The local CCF party faithful were very devoted to him and proud to work for him as their candidate. There was unparalleled loyalty on the part of the volunteers in the local riding office. My parents found an affection among these people which was as strong as family. But there were just not enough of them to make a difference to his vote.

The cost of a campaign, according to the Woodsworth House papers, University of Toronto archives, was $800.00, not much, perhaps, by today's standards, but a fortune in my parents' eyes at the time. When Conservative George Hees ran a moneyed campaign in 1950, it was not surprising that my father lost to him. What was a blow to George was that the Liberal candidate who came in second was a student who had failed her college History course.

George did not really like being a political candidate; he hated the "popularity contest" aspect of it. In some ways, he had had too different and difficult a life to be "one of the boys." When he was elected to the Board of Education in 1941, it was in recognition of his intelligence and expertise as an educator. George threw himself into this work for the next three years. He decided to make a list on April

10, 1941 of all the matters requiring his attention. He planned to visit all public schools in his ward. Why were auxiliary classes for slow learners being closed? He made a point of meeting all the instructors of such special classes, and found them "a very lively bunch of teachers -- more alive than the ordinary run. They have to be." (April 30, 1942 diary) He soon was chairman of the Special Schools committee.

Through many letters, telephone calls, and visits to schools, he set up a hot lunch cafeteria program for the whole city. He did his research carefully, seeing which schools would have to rely on facilities nearby. It took a monumental effort to put the program in place. As one supporter put it, England in time of war could look after its children, so Canada which was not being bombarded should be able to. In the secondary schools, children would choose the lunch program over the recreational program because they really needed the nutrition. The cost of the hot lunch program plus daycare before and after school was 25 cents a day and 10 cents for each additional child in the same family.

Keeping up the daycare program also took an enormous amount of work. If it were not completed, women would make less satisfactory arrangements. As it was wartime, every woman had to apply to the Selective Service authorities in person to ensure her work was deemed essential. George was concerned that less responsible parents would not make the effort. He wanted daycare open to all mothers employed outside the home. Ten new daycare centres were opened on his insistence, and George told the *Toronto Star* on June 23, 1943: "It is impossible to draw the line between essential and non-essential in wartime....Children should not pay the price." Trained volunteers from the Women's Voluntary Services plus local volunteers worked in the centres before and after school. It was difficult to find women willing to volunteer, so providing carfare was recommended as an incentive. Community co-operation from such city organizations as the Jarvis School for Boys, the Children's Art Centre, the Workmen's Compensation Clinic, YMCA and church groups supplied 74 pieces of play equipment.

Then there was his work as chairman of the Farm Service Committee. Neither George nor the school principals cared for the redefinition of farm work in section 27 to include working in a creamery, factory, cannery or food-processing plant, and he got them to endorse a condemnation of such an unhealthy redefinition. Children should only be released to help on the farms, and even then they were not to go until the end of May. These students were after all still children who should be in school. George thought that during the period they promised to work on the farms, they should even have a one-week vacation for the sake of their health.

There were other matters he wanted to work on. Classes were very crowded in those days. George urged the opening of another Grade 8 class at Queen Alexandra school since there were fifty in the existing class. The inspection system was obviously not working in the secondary schools. Were the reports on teachers available to the Board? He must find out. Another matter that concerned him was that a family could not receive a man's pension even if he died after 10-15 years service. He must look into initiating a pension scheme. He was interested in the work of the Property Committee. What were the estimated cuts? There were so many items that needed attention. New Canadians should be able to take language classes in the schools in the evenings. And in the middle of it all he had to get over the hurdle of an election on New Year's Day.

On March 19, 1943, the *Telegram* wrote that George had introduced a resolution to open the school facilities to languages other than English. The University College French Dramatics Society had tried to rent a school auditorium. The resolution exploded like a bomb in the Toronto of 1943. George had to quickly change it. He was a practical man; there was no sense in banging one's head against a stone wall. There were other resolutions he wanted to get through. By the end of his 3 years on the board, he had accomplished an amazing amount. The names of those who slowed his progress rang like the clangs of devils throughout our house: Superintendent of Education Goldring, and representatives Isabel Ross and May Birchard.

The reason for the enormous energy George could turn to such activity as his work on the Board of Education was his emotional commitment to whatever he was working on. He writes about the issue of no daycare for non-essential war work of mothers:

> *The most pathetic case is probably that of a child whose mother is in a mental home, and whose father works. It [the father's work] too is classified as non-essential....The whole basis of selection seems quite unsatisfactory.*

In the middle of this period of working so hard for the Toronto Board of Education, he accuses himself of lack of persistence. Just as he would get in line to have a very important position for a sustained length of time, he would remove himself or get removed from that organization. "Perhaps my secret ambition to be a writer is the only fulfilment that might bring the sense of work well done," he writes on April 24, 1942, in a rough diary he kept on the back of a manuscript. He was thinking of writing a book on democracy and he mused that it would have to contain certain elements: the faith in the common man, for every man had a soul and there were limits expected from the ordinary man in a democracy. Politics was the kingly science but the reality was that pressure groups were necessary and there were elections to be held. He continues on April 30, 1942: "The LSR [League for Social Reconstruction] was of great interest. I swore it had a function, refused to see the signs of decay. I was made president in 1941. I have done nothing whatever since, not even answered letters."

It was the same with the *Canadian Forum*. Through 1938 and 1939, he produced it almost single-handed. "When the war came, I dropped it; the war made it inadvisable for me to carry on alone." In 1940, he took on similar responsibilities with the paper *The Commonwealth*. He worked at it "like a galley slave and gave it up when I was elected to the Board of Education in January '42." As for the books he had written on Plato and Euripides, "All the verve had gone before I finished it. The finishing was just self-discipline." He thought the lack of persistence was based in part on the puritanical influence of his mother, her sainthood according to the rest of his family. He admired his father who was very successful with women and wanted to be just like him. Whatever his ambition had been as a child professionally, he had, generally speaking, already accomplished. He had, at that moment, no overriding interest in any one direction. "I am, it is true, still capable of great concentration upon restricted ends, articles, speeches, lectures, or getting a particular measure through."(Oct. 11, '42) He felt that all he was doing was "Just wandering about the cave setting a few things right here and there. Too much detail and no master plan."

Much of his energy came from his putting himself with enthusiasm into what he was working on. This is evident, for example, in the speech he gave to a Labour-Zionist Convention in 1943. He identified with his audience. Without actually saying he's speaking of himself, he claimed, "It is possible for individuals to tear themselves away from their roots -- *un déraciné* -- it is possible for the overintellectualized... to live a worthwhile life." He expressed the deep interest and sympathy of his Party for their work. He assured his audience that a socialist government would work for legislation against the worst external expressions of prejudice. He praised the contributions of the Jewish settlements in Palestine and said how thrilling it was to read of cities like Tel Aviv rising from the wilderness. He ended by speaking of the cultural and spiritual contribution of all religions or cultural or racial groups rooted in history and tradition.

How did George manage to do twice the activities of most men? He knew he had the tendency to do too much. January 3, 1944 found him writing in a few pages of rough diary that he was beginning the year as usual in a jam. The CCF pulled him one way -- it always had a high place on his agenda -- and other meetings pulled him another. He enjoyed delivering speeches, and had just completed one on Social Services for a CCF educational conference. There were always lectures and classes to prepare on top of everything else. Despite all his hard work for the Board, because he was part of the CCF slate in the January 1, 1945 election, he was defeated. But if he kept up his present pace -- this week he had 2 board meetings, an executive meeting, a conference at Queen's Park, and an executive meeting in Ottawa on Saturday -- he "would know less at the end of the year than the beginning" he wrote. He chastises himself for missing a Faculty council meeting. He thought of running for chairman of the board but knows that he "does more good as an ordinary member. All very amusing but it takes too much time."

There were other, less tangible reasons for his not winning any future elections. During the war years, there was in Canada a great suspicion of anyone born on the Continent. Unlike Britain and the United States, Canada denied access to professionals from Europe, though she desperately needed them. Most Canadians know about the expulsion of the Japanese from the west coast, but few are aware of the internment of Jewish professionals, and even fewer know of the denial of admission to Polish engineers and professionals -- a very different policy from today's attitude to refugees. Like today, however, the less education people had, the greater their intolerance of those from elsewhere. Toronto's East End was so full of uneducated people, mostly of British origin, that no one with a foreign name could have won an election there. Then there were the rural areas of Ontario that George was addressing as president of the CCF in the early '40s. Rural Ontario was intolerant of the CCF, unlike during the First World War when it elected the United Farmers representatives. Parts of it were very Protestant, so that as late as the 1950s a teacher was fired for practicing golf in her back garden of a Sunday morning. A free-thinking atheistic professor got nowhere at all with such farmers and townsfolk.

Another reason for his lack of success as a candidate was that as he got older he tended to present to the world a fiercer public personality than he really had. Many have told me how intimidating they found him. Certainly he was not the type to look as if he enjoyed -- nor did he enjoy -- the day-to-day social whirl of electioneering.

He had some successes on the Board of Education. With him were fellow socialists Tmima Cohen and Ted Davidson. The three of them persuaded the Board to give municipal scholarships at the age of 16 to needy students who were academically promising. They asked for ten thousand dollars for these scholarships and got three thousand. The Board members themselves worked without pay. They introduced hot lunches, but as soon as the CCFers were defeated in 1944, the Board said they'd get rid of that waste of money. They couldn't. The public wouldn't allow it. In 1949, my father ran one more time for the Board of Education but was defeated. In 1944, my mother Gwenyth had also run but was also defeated.

When he tried to proceed to federal politics, he was unsuccessful. He said he preferred political educating between elections, such as writing pamphlets or drafting convention resolutions, to the heat of an election battle itself. When Toronto's East End riding of Broadview changed its ethnic component to Greek many years later in the 1970s, it voted socialist and put Lynn Macdonald in as its representative. It happened that George's last vote in 1982 was from Riverdale hospital and he was able to help vote in a socialist candidate in the riding he had run in 30 years before. The nurse asked him while he was voting if he was sure he knew what he was doing! He must have answered with great firmness for apparently she came out very red-faced.

When George ran in a by-election in 1949, Trinity College's Board of Governors, mindful of the stir with the provincial government ten years earlier, tried to impose certain guidelines for him to sign. Provost Cosgrave, the same provost who had defended him ten years previously, wanted no recurrence of trouble. As George was eating supper at the College High Table three consecutive nights, he and Cosgrave had exactly the same conversation each night. Provost Cosgrave addressed him with "Are you interested in this election?" Each time George replied, "Yes, I'm a candidate, you know." The Provost would continue that he had heard something to that effect. It was his way of rebuking George for not having asked his permission to be a candidate. George had consulted him the first time he ran for parliament in 1940. (Robin Harris' interview, Trinity and University of Toronto archives p. 45) Provost Cosgrave would say something like "Don't you think these people are exploiting you?," to which George would reply, "Mr. Provost, I'm the President of the [provincial] Party. What do you mean they're exploiting me?" And this went on for some time, but because the two men, both strong individuals, respected each other, they kept control over their tempers.

The Executive of Trinity College wanted the Provost to have George sign a paper that said he had taken into account the organization to which he belonged. When George asked him, "Does this mean I have done anything wrong? Because if it does, I won't sign it," he replied, "No. No. No." Finally George said, "Well, it's not usual to sign instructions. I will receive them, but if I don't obey them, you can take measures." Such reasonableness must have infuriated those on the Trinity Executive who were trying to intimidate him, but luckily his immediate superior the Provost was not one of those. Because Cosgrave respected him, George was very loyal to both his job and his college. If he ever had been elected, he would have had to give up his academic career. His college had been his life, far more than just a job. His office was where he did his creative thinking. It provided him with the peace of mind to make his writing possible. He liked to balance this privileged life with the contact with the variety of people in the CCF.

In 1941, George became the first President of the Ontario CCF. Part of the reason he was elected to this post was his public speaking ability. His timetable of public speaking to CCF rallies, picnics and meetings was exhausting. Yet he managed to do it all during the times he was not teaching. In spite of the many speaking engagements, he never missed a single class. His bilingualism meant he could address groups of French Canadian miners in their own language, though mastery of both of Canada's official languages was not the boost to success in Federal politics that it would have been today. Even though he was extremely busy, for he also served as a member of the national CCF Executive, he obviously enjoyed this involvement. To George both politics and academics were his work. He writes on April 23, 1944:

> *That I would be elected president of the Ontario CCF was a foregone conclusion. I told everyone that I want to travel and see the movement -- to establish contact between headquarters and the membership. I'll need a card index to*

remember names and faces.... I wish I could take pictures of them all.

He then underlined the names in an effort to remember them. He writes of the contrast between "two old timers, argumentative socialists, true people but not willing to accept the new membership. The future obviously needs the younger set. We want to make a synthesis between the two."

The main factor of the times which made politics different from what it is today was that politics was enjoyment. Political speeches were a good form of entertainment. Toronto had little professional theatre in the early '40s, except for the occasional visiting show at the Royal Alexandra Theatre, and not many restaurants of note except La Chaumière, a favourite of my father's. There was the Art Gallery and the Royal Ontario Museum and many went there of a Sunday afternoon as they were the only places open. In our family, it was my mother who took us there. My father never rallied us for a Sunday outing; we always presumed he was too busy with his work. In the '30s and early '40s we occasionally went to a Sunday tea at a CCFer's. Earl and Esther Birney's and Tmima Cohen's come to mind. Or we might stop in on a CCF family with my mother.

George really enjoyed hosting a party, much to the surprise of those who knew him as a formidable professor. My parents' specialty was an evening party or an informal cocktail party. My parents didn't give dinner parties, although they often had people in to share the family meal. My mother did not consider herself a cook. After all, in her youth in London, there were servants in middle-class households to do the cooking. According to Mary Millard, there were CCF dinner parties, but that may have been among what Mary called "the above-Bloor crowd," which we certainly were not.

In the summer my parents liked to entertain at their Ward's Island cottage. In the '50s M. J. Coldwell, who was leader of the CCF for many years, came there every September to spend a week's holiday. The Island was then at its best: the nights were cool and the days good for walking. The weather was still pleasant, but there were no crowds coming to the beaches. Usually, we would have a fire in the evenings. My memory is of M. J. (as we and many others called him) sitting by the fire in an old, comfortable wicker chair having tea, and obviously enjoying his holiday immensely. He was such a nice gentleman that we were all pleased to have him with us. When I had my first teaching job in Ottawa, he had me to a tea served very simply by his housekeeper. When I got married, he sent a charming linen tablecloth. In a letter with no date M. J. wrote to my parents of the camaraderie he enjoyed among political friends: "I look back to the old CCF with affection for the idealism, the comradeship and the loyalty which you both, many others and I found in it." (Box 1 Trinity Archives)

In the fifties, according to George in his review of Leo Zakuta's *A Protest Movement Becalmed* (*Commentator* Nov. 1964), the CCF could go on acting as a major party and at the same time retain a good deal of its crusading spirit. George was still at the helm of many of his socialist activities. In a speech in Sudbury the April after the founding of the New Party, he stated: "The CCF was a socialist party. The New Democratic Party will take socialist measures when necessary." His basic faith remained unwavering as he continued accusing other parties of vacillating with respect to defense policy: "We are the only party who have stated clearly we are against acceptance of nuclear weapons in this country."

All the CCFers who have been elevated to a kind of sainthood -- J. S. Woodsworth, Tommy Douglas, M. J. Coldwell -- came from west of Ontario. From my experience of living many years in Vancouver I would say we're very good at nostalgia in the west. Agnes MacPhail, the leader of the Farmers' Progressive Movement, was the only woman in Parliament with the possibility of a peek in at sainthood, but generally Ontario does not go in for this sort of thing. When she was bored, she apparently used to take out her nail file. She must have had very well-kept nails. As Mary Millard said, "Ontario is not good at saints." There are no grants to make videos about the lives of Ontario socialists. Quite the reverse. My parents who were devoted CCFers all their lives only became Life Members -- an honour bestowed by the party -- in their late seventies. They would not have wanted it otherwise. For them the important thing was to get on with the job of bringing socialism to the province. Margaret Sedgewick Lazaros, who gave her whole professional life as well as all her voluntary time to the party, went into her local NDP office at the time of the 1965 election and no one had heard of her. Donald MacDonald writes in the preface of *The Happy Warrior* that there is no history written about Ontario socialism. Rosemay Speirs makes the same point in her book *Out of the Blue*. My brother, John Grube, claimed that Donald Creighton told him the reason for no history of Ontario being written was that the history of Ontario is the history of Canada. Whether this is just a happy-sounding phrase if you live in Ontario or in fact true I am not historian enough to judge.

Although George received a salary for only his academic job, his political activity was every bit as important to him as his professorship. Within the family we were very aware of this, for it would be just as serious to interrupt him when he was in a political meeting as when he was working on a scholarly article. Since he devoted so much time to his political work, he had little time to devote to the writing of books which would have earned him money much needed by our family in the 1940s. For some years he earned a little extra by teaching the summer school elementary Greek which he enjoyed since the students took it because they wanted to rather than just doing a required course. Once or twice he gave extension courses in Classics.

The interesting fact is that he accomplished more than one man might in both his academic and political work. It was as if the one activity gave him energy for the other. In both fields his emotions were engaged as well as his intellect. When he dedicated his book *Plato's Thought* to his teacher R. Cary Gilson in 1935, he wrote that the dedication was an offering, since Gilson had "opened for me the golden gates." To be engaged enthusiastically in scholarship and to be inspired by it was to see the light.

What he enjoyed most in his political work was not the running for political office, but chairing conventions. Apparently he was very good at it. He used to say it was like conducting an orchestra to give every person his fair share of time. According to Grace MacInnis (June 1988 interview), "He was very fair, even giving the Communists their share of time." When he came home, he would curse them as "those damn Trotskyites," for he considered them the true enemies of socialism, and a real pain in the neck on the convention floor. He viewed the political spectrum as a circle with the ultra-right and the ultra-left meeting at the top. In other words, the doctrine of the one extreme was really like that of the other, and he had little use for Communists, whom he saw as just occupants of the opposite extreme from the ultra-right Conservatives or Fascists.

He told his former student and political colleague, Margaret Lazaros, that the secret of chairmanship was to talk naturally (interview by Margaret Lazaros and Mary Millard, Woodsworth House papers, Box 75, University of Toronto archives). Only 300 people made up the conventions of his day compared to the thousands of today. There was a more intimate atmosphere and he could make a joke when he felt like it. When an objectional little man who was always at the microphone said, "I have been standing here for 20 minutes," George made a remark typical of his kind of irony, "Well, it's time you sat down then."

He also acted naturally in expressing his annoyance if he felt like it. At one convention in the late fifties, he got very annoyed at a man named Peters, the representative from Sudbury, and at Hazen Argue, whom he found a nuisance and a windbag on the convention floor and he didn't mince words in letting him know it. George's stern demeanour helped in creating an atmosphere where he was rarely challenged as a chairman. He gave the convention floor the impression that everything had been intellectually thought out; only his family knew how much he did business on the spur of the moment.

The intensity of conventions in that era was due to the fact that politics, however enjoyable it might be as a "spectator sport," was, for those deeply involved, a very serious business. The convention in Ontario was an arena where the CCF was fighting for its political life against the Communists. The chairman had a high profile in conducting resolutions through in a harmonious way, without creating trouble that the press could easily magnify. One of the reasons delegates went to a convention was to be inspired, so that they could go back to their ridings with renewed energy. Speakers like Tommy Douglas and Stanley Knowles with their experience as preachers could create a messianic atmosphere. The job of the chairman was to facilitate this and not create artificial battles by provoking challenges that interfered with the setting of policy. The record number of resolutions passed when he was chairman was 107. (Univ. of Toronto Archives) Mary Millard, a party worker all her life, felt surprise when other chairmen came to the fore, as she had presumed everyone could do it with the ease that my father did. George managed to get through a great number of resolutions. He shepherded them through and cut off people politely. He may have appeared to do it with ease, but chairing did take it out of him. During one week-end convention, in the late forties, the tension was so great that he fainted Sunday morning before he went off to spend the day chairing. He acted that day with a little more restraint, but only our family knew how the day had begun.

As chairman, and especially as one from Toronto, he was sometimes resented. As one young Ottawa CCF worker said to me in 1958 when I was teaching there, "I'm not going to bother to go to the convention. Why should I hear some bugger from Toronto railroading resolutions through?"

Chapter 6:
The Canadian Forum

As well as being on committees and serving as chairman, George contributed a great deal to *The Canadian Forum.* It had started in the early 1920s with Barker Fairley. *The Forum* (as it was then known) had arisen from "The Stafford Printers." Margaret Lazaros said her husband Morden was one of the prime movers. His object was a socialist press. Originally, Graham Spry had started a newspaper, *The New Commonwealth,* which published only one issue. When they bought the printing press for $1 and called the publication *The Stafford Press,* they hoped for some sort of endowment from the British socialist Sir Stafford Cripps. To their surprise, all they received from Sir Stafford was a cheery letter and a five-pound note. The *Press* met on Sherbourne Street in the middle of the old Saint Paul's riding. George was a leading figure at this busy place. While we went up to Muskoka to escape the heat of Toronto summers, he would toil away in the hot Sherbourne Street office. He had a hand in writing the leaflets which they distributed about the CCF. The *Stafford Press* people were broadening their scope, and to attract a wider audience, they changed their title to *The Forum.* Always an avid reader, George first became involved in writing book reviews. Soon he was a driving force behind the publication. From 1935 to 1939, he served on the editorial board, along with such notables as Frank Underhill and Earl Birney. When George became editor in 1937, the magazine was in the red, but he boasted he managed to get it into the black during his time as editor. In 1935, Carlton "Bill" McNaught promised $1000, the LSR committed $200, and Jacob Markowitz, a doctor, promised $40 a month. In 1938, George's fellow Classicist from Victoria College, Eric Havelock, had the idea of a sustaining fund to which people might be encouraged to donate. The circulation went from 900 to 3000 by 1942. In the early 1940s, when George thought the publication would reach more people if his name were removed from the masthead because he was by then president of the Ontario CCF, this was done, though many could still recognize his writing. George wrote that he was unwilling to hide his opinions or to try to steer clear of controversy. He didn't want to do the work in wartime. He felt a Canadian-born editor should be found: "... there is no point giving the adversary a handle he is sure to use with some effect." In any case, *The Forum* now needed a full-time editor. He supposed an Englishman might be all right as editor, but his own preference was for a Canadian. In further writing, he used a pseudonym, Max Reiners, shortening one of his middle names, Maximilien to Max and using his mother's maiden name Reiners as surname.

Certain opinions came through repeatedly in his writing: his admiration for the British Labour Party; his dislike of Communist Party tactics; his unwavering belief in socialism; the inspiration he drew from the Classics. By writing in such a journal, he could reach a wider audience than by addressing socialist meetings or lecturing to university classes. Because he thought that a man could not be just an observer of life's events but should be a participant, he felt he had a duty to communicate with as large a public as possible. Even in his book reviews, he emphasized the importance of clarity in writing. In his writings in *The Forum*, in his home, to his students and to people he knew, he often said that anybody could write in a florid manner, but it took a clear mind to write in a simple and straightforward style.

Certain themes were important to him. One was the attitude CCFers should take to Communism. Like other academics, he had been more willing to listen to them in the mid-1930s. In a letter to Frank Underhill (July 23, 1936), he wrote:

> *Personally, I am getting fed up with this blind party refusal to co-operate with any Communists at least on local issues. As you know I've been chafing under it for a year. I don't mind remaining loyal if they will only recognize that they must take notice of new situations in other countries. I find the Garland attitude quite impossible to swallow, and I'm quite sure that in the end it's suicidal.*
>
> *(Underhill Papers Public Archives, Ottawa)*

Yet a year later, due to his strong aversion to Stalinist tactics, he tried in *The Forum* to persuade socialists that Communism was their worst enemy. He quoted Norman Thomas, the American socialist presidential candidate whom I remember as an impressive eminence grise at our table when he came to address a meeting in Toronto. While Communists preached a united front against fascism, they themselves were intensifying suspicion, division, and mutual hatred in the working-class movements of the world. Emphasizing that the confessions at these trials were probably false, George warned that there was in Soviet Russia "an autocracy as completely unscrupulous as it is ruthless in its persecution." ("Moscow Trials," *The Forum*, March 1937)

Like many Canadian socialists, though not averse to criticizing British socialism, he had an absorbing interest in it. Because the famous English socialist, G. D. H. Cole, whom my father also entertained in our home, glossed over "the difficulties of Soviet Communism" and took "a somewhat enthusiastic view of liberty in Russia," George rebuked him (*The Forum* book review, July 1937). He thought it reprehensible that Leopold Infeld, a Canadian scientist and professor of some distinction at the University of Toronto, after the war returned to live in Poland, a Communist society, just because the country he had left as a poor boy had given him the royal treatment when he visited it as a scientist. In another review six years later, "Britain in the World Front" (*The Forum*, Feb. 1943), George expressed the same disapproval of those who closed their eyes to the failure of Communism: "It is indeed a pity that the author cannot discard the Communist habit of ignoring inconvenient facts." He criticized even the possibility of allowing Communists or fellow travellers as union organizers. That would involve a conflict of loyalty to one's union and to the CCF. He never hesitated to point out to Canadians the bad habit British Labourites had of being blind to the dangers of associating with Communists. George was a fervent supporter of the British Labour Party itself. He felt that Canada should recognize and incorporate trade unions and other labour organizations, as the British Labour Party had. In his review of another of G. D. H. Cole's books, *British Working Class Politics 1832-1914,* George accused Canada of still being in the 19th century with respect to trade-union and labour organizations: "We still have a tremendous lot to learn from events in Britain, particularly in the fifty years before the last war." (*The Forum*, May 1941) He suggested that Canadians could well "look to Britain in its recognition of the power of Parliament." In reviewing Helen P. Kirkpatrick's *Under the British Umbrella* (*The Forum*, Feb. 1940), George wrote that when Britain declared war, "Parliament had suddenly discovered that it was a powerful organ, the representative of public opinion. Would that as much could be said for Canada." In treating Labour as a partner in the war effort and not as a "dangerous nuisance to be put off with promises and as little action as necessary," Britain accomplished more. ("What Labour Needs," *The Forum*, May 1941) Because Canada did not make use of its unions as a power but rather tried to brush them aside with false promises, Canada was, in George's opinion, years behind Britain. If Canadians did not have the right to strike, they would be, unlike Britain in similar circumstances, "living under a system of economic feudalism before the war was over, with the worst type of employer dictating, not only to workers but to the government itself."

These articles show George as an Anglophile, so it was ironic that, in 1939, Premier Hepburn and Opposition Leader George Drew should have accused him of being anti-British. He found a great deal of inspiration from his life in Britain and from the British example. Up to the Second World War, he returned to Britain every summer term, and based his teaching on his Cambridge education. In his fifties and sixties, he went to Britain a number of times. It was the real Britain, not the abstraction that Drew was talking about, some vague fairyland ideal.

Since the European Continent was his heritage and he had spent the first fourteen years of his life in Belgium, he also found inspiration from writings from the Continent. He felt strongly that Canadians could increase their understanding of the First World War by reading certain French books available in translation, such as *The League Fiasco* by Y. Margueritte, and *Collective Security* by Maurice Bourquouin. (*The Forum*, Jan. 1937) Books like these would, in his view, give readers a chance to see the French point of view. This made them "of greater value to the British reader."

It is interesting that George used the term "British" to cover both British and British Canadian. He enjoyed poking fun at British (and presumably British Canadian) reserve in his review of Gabriel Chevalier's novel about French village life, *Clochemerle*. (*The Forum*, Feb. 1937) Clochemerle is a zesty, amusing, and delightfully 'low' portrayal of paysan humour: for example, the local doctor cures one of his female patient's constipation by having a number of hearty souls sit on her stomach. George, as a Continental, remarked that comparing the French and English versions would make "a good starting point for a study of the perverted reticences of the Anglo-Saxon."

In an article entitled “Civil Liberties in Wartime” (July 1940), he warned of what he discerned in Canada as a threat to civil liberties. The real danger "lies in the unscrupulous fanning of racial antagonisms against Canadians of 'foreign' origin. That is a menace to the unity of this country of which we must beware. And it may be as well to remember that Hitler's most effective agents are not poor devils without a coat to their backs." He warned Canadians but did not set himself apart as being separate in any way. He often wrote "we" when a small intellegentsia would be the only possible people agreeing with him, but he does not think in terms of "they".

To say that someone's thinking was just like Aristotle's was to criticize it, in George's view. When reviewing Lord Lloyd's *The British Case: a Contrast*, June 1940, he disputed the philosophy that all men have to be governed except those in a small and homogeneous community with common interests. With Lord Lloyd, he thought "we should attempt to give new expression to the directing idea which, last time, led to the League of Nations."

Another target of his satire was the self-satisfied confidence that he thought many Christians showed. He found John Hoyland's *Digging for a New England* particularly corrective of this confidence. He recommended it to all "contented Christians. It should give them a lot of sleepless nights." (*The Forum*, Aug. 1936) It would be good for many Christians to find they didn't have all the answers, he thought. In his review of W. D. Stewart's *Dictatorship or Democracy*, although he agreed with the author's call for a new morality, he doubted whether this would come through the Churches or outside them, but indeed in spite of them. (*The Forum,* July 1939) Yet, when a very devout Christian neighbour at our summer cottage referred to him as one of the finest Christian gentlemen of her acquaintance, he was amused and pleased at the compliment. Although she knew he was an agnostic, this was the most complimentary phrase in her vocabulary.

George's humour often hit the mark. In reviewing Harold Nicolson's *Small Talk* and reflecting on the title of the book, he suggested there should be a Ministry of Things of No Importance to do "for our comfort the thousand things we can agree on but for which our politicians have no time." This book, he continued, was a literary counterpart to that Ministry. (*The Forum*, Sept. 1937)

We have caught a glimpse of George Grube, the anti-Communist, the Anglophile yet Continental, and the pithy humorist. In his *Forum* articles, there was also George Grube, the very certain socialist, the Classicist, and the civil libertarian. In 1941, in an article entitled "Labor and the Government," he wrote that economic-planned organization was the burning need. Trade-unionists were much more aware of this, he wrote, than was Mr. King or his government. (*The Forum*, March 1941) "At last the workers are on the march. The path is not made easy for them -- that is the more reason that they should speak, not only industrially but politically." He reflected the optimism that the socialists felt about the politicization of Canadian workers. George was convinced Canada was on the road to socialism. On the other hand, he also recognized the terrific odds that the unions faced. In an article written in October 1942, he wrote that the government believed that the best way to negotiate was to wield a big club. While the workers' representatives were in Ottawa in negotiations with the government, the same government was betraying them with an injunction against them.

George was not one to just point out a problem without also putting forward a solution. He suggested steps for progress in the recognition of the power of labour in Canada in an article, "Wanted:

a Minister of Labor." (*The Forum*, July 1942) The government should revoke its power under the National Defence Act to call out the army in order to break up a strike. Working people should be free to negotiate with employers through their freely chosen representatives. Government employees should have the right to organize. There should be a minimum wage. Workers should receive bonuses on a uniform basis. There should be effective guarantees against victimization and discrimination. Organized labour should have representation on production and control boards. Many of these suggestions we have come to accept as given, others are still disputed.

In the early nineteen-forties particularly, the socialists had the feeling they were going to achieve their aims in Canada. Esther Birney described to me the optimism that was generated in their meetings. They felt they really were going to change the country. The working class through the enlightenment of education was going to become socialists in just a matter of time. However, socialism in Ontario was to take a very different turn. In 1943, the CCF did fairly well, although George lost as the CCF candidate in the federal election in Broadview. In 1944, the Ontario government along with the business community feared the socialists would win. With the knowledge of several cabinet ministers, big business paid for professional propagandists to slur the names of prominent CCFers in Ontario. It put an ad in the *Toronto Telegram* on the eve of the election accusing them of being Communists and saying George was the president of the Communist party. It also accused William Dennison, later mayor of Toronto. The *Globe* ran the same ad the next morning and there was no time for a reasoned response before the election.

For some time, the police had been shadowing respectable men and women. Even cabinet ministers had known about this but had done nothing to stop such tactics. Jolliffe and Wismer, top Executive men on the Ontario provincial CCF Council, decided to stage a rebuttal without consulting others on the Executive. For one thing, there was no time for consultation. They got Lister Sinclair to dramatize the event in a radio script which accused the government of Gestapo tactics; they were sure the Ontario public would be outraged. What in fact happened was that the CCF Executive were taken by surprise and business men, cabinet officials, and the general public were caught off guard. According to Mary Millard, a CCF organizer at the time, Lister Sinclair's radio script made the story seem more fiction than fact and gave the whole incident an air of unreality. A young man at Queen's University who was doing some research had come upon the detailed papers of how the police had carried out their investigation and the instructions that had been given them. Ontario voters, conservative by nature, were annoyed at the socialists for bringing such unpleasant tactics to their attention. They voted overwhelmingly against the CCF. The only CCF-sponsored candidate in the Toronto area to survive the frenzied advertising campaign was Mary Endicott (wife of James G. Endicott; see p. 162 of the book *James G. Endicott* written by his son, Stephen) and others doubt whether the CCF actually sponsored her.

The Tory firm which had led the campaign was called Reliable Exterminators Inc. The socialists referred to M. A. Sanderson, the man leading it, as the Bug Man. Everyone was upset: big business was furious because the CCF had exposed their tactics; the police were angry since some of their officials had behaved improperly; the members of the Ontario public didn't want anything to do with politics that smacked of being investigated; the CCFers whom the two members of the Executive had not consulted about their method of counterattack felt betrayed. Wismer and Jolliffe were distressed that their response had not had the effect of getting people outraged at the injustice and of turning that into CCF votes.

Despite all efforts, however, the upsurge of the CCF in central Canada was over for a long time, mainly due to hostile propaganda.

In *The Forum* for June 1945, George wrote of a "new low in Canadian political life." That cabinet ministers were involved particularly upset him. He felt these were people who had earned the respect of the community, in whom it had put its trust. Yet such ministers had "stooped to a deliberate and provocative falsehood." Secondly, the actions of the police disturbed him. In December of the same year, he wrote of his reactions to the Lebel Commission inquiry. In his article entitled "The Lebel Report and Civil Liberties," he wrote that something rotten had taken place at Police Headquarters, since "high officials in the police let an investigation be carried out with the purpose of campaigning against the CCF, a party in opposition." As it was a junior officer who helped bring the matter to the attention of the politicians who were being maligned, my father remarked that "the higher the official the less good his recall of the details of the case." With vigour, George proposed a solution: "It is up to the Legislature and the people of this province to see that this rotten blot upon the credit of our police force is cleared up once and for all." It is typical of his fair-mindedness that he did not blame the whole police force, but rather wanted to see the majority's name cleared of the actions of a few. A libel suit ensued with Andrew Brewin of Toronto and John Cartwright of Kingston as prosecutors. The jury consisted of important business people who were usually exempt from jury duty. Since those running the ad had been financed by big business, it was obviously a fixed outcome. In spite of this, the CCFers won the trial and received the expenses of the trial plus $1.00 in damages from the one paper and 1 cent from the other.

Another reason the CCF did so poorly in this election was that the federal and provincial elections were within a week of each other, and as a party they just didn't have the funds to conduct two campaigns within such a short time. After receiving her B.A. from the University of Toronto, Mary Millard took charge of three important ridings at this time: St. George, St. Patrick, and St. Paul. She ran three campaigns from one room. In order to get three candidates, the CCF tried to get people to run as both provincial and federal candidates. The CCF did better in the provincial election in 1948 than in the 1945 fiasco.

The sort of political contribution George did enjoy was being chairman of the CCF's research committee. Research and education between elections was much more to his liking than campaigning. George had the ability to see the whole picture. Perhaps the Classicist in him was responsible for this clarity of vision. In reviewing *Mixed Company* by J.C. Robertson (*The Forum*, April 1940), he wrote of the charm and fascination that Greek thought and Greek culture had had on thinkers for two thousand years. The *Iliad* was one of the world's greatest stories, a pattern for all time of the story-teller's art, my father noted. Continuing his praise, he extolled "the vivid freshness of Homer, his amazing ability to make the past and the future part of the present, the skilful use of suspense and delayed action, his imagery, the building of character from the action itself." Perhaps reading widely in a civilization like the Greek gave my father a kind of optimism. A great age could come again. One must work towards that both intellectually and politically.

Writing and speaking style was always of great importance to him. In his early *Forum* writings, in reviewing Freud's *An Autobiographical Study*, he stated the gist of what I heard him often say in a conversational way: "It is the gift of the really great, especially in humanistic studies, to be less obscure than smaller men and to be free from unnecessary technical jargon." Years later, in his book *The Greek and Roman Critics* (Toronto 1965), he sided with the recommendation of the Greek critic on style Dionysius of

Halicarnassus: "Always use current, simple language without tropes or elaboration" (p. 213). The Roman poet Horace was not as casual as his style suggests, for behind it is a systematic structure of ideas (p. 240). George used to claim that it took a great author to write simply and clearly. His own object was that everyone, not just the Classical scholar, be able to understand him. In fact, he thought of himself as a popularizer. He was pleased that his translation of Plato's *Republic* was a bestseller on college campuses. Ken Bryden, one-time socialist organizer and later professor of Political Science at the University of Toronto, said he realized that George had succeeded in making his books available to all when he saw one in an airport bookstore.

George believed in the power that humanistic studies had. The humanist, unlike the mathematician, could improve with age. In 1959-60, when George was 60, he held a Guggenheim Fellowship for $5000 for one-half year at the Institute for Advanced Studies at Princeton, New Jersey. He used to say that mathematicians had reached the pinnacle of success in their mid-twenties; the humanists at the Institute were all in their sixties. As he saw it, because the humanist had accumulated wisdom with age, it was his duty to be concerned with the public good. In a *Forum* review of Henry Nevinson's *The Fire of Life*, George praised the author: "Like Odysseus of old, he has seen the lands of many men and understood their minds. Here is a man to whom the public good is the very breath of life and his (own) successes, failures or ailments only of minor interest." Only the broken man does not take on his public duty. In reviewing Jean Tousseul's *Jean Clarambaux* (*The Forum*, Jan. 1940), my father put it this way: "Jean is a broken man; gardening and raising chickens is not the answer to the world's problems; for a man such as he is supposed to have been, it is only a subtle form of self-indulgence." That a man with great potential should busy himself with only his own concerns did not impress George. As he saw it, such a man was merely being selfish in not doing his duty.

It is interesting to find so many of George's concerns and beliefs reflected throughout his contributions to *The Forum*. Certainly, the themes that appeared again and again in my father's articles and book reviews from 1937 to 1950 were the concerns he spoke of with conviction: a man's public duty; the importance of the Classics; a condemnation of the Communists and their efforts to obscure socialism; Canadian socialism getting inspiration from the British Labour Party, and socialism as the answer to Canada's problems.

In his book *The League for Social Reconstruction,* Michiel Horn labeled George a pacifist, apparently on the basis of an article in *The Forum*. Does this charge have any basis in fact? His articles in *The Forum* trace his change of heart on this subject. In 1936, he took a pacifist position and urged Canada to abstain from the build-up of armaments in Europe. In May 1938, he wanted Canadians to decide in Parliament whether they would go to war in support of Britain. By October 1938 he advised Canadians to look to creating peace in their own country first. In November 1939, he objected to the use of the War Measures Act in an article "Freedom and War." As a socialist, he preferred implementing social services to waging war. In January 1940 he acknowledged that Hitlerism was the enemy wherever it existed. He urged opposition to the forces of tyranny "in our own country." Neither I, nor either of my siblings when I consulted them, ever thought of him as a pacifist when we knew him. No doubt, as anyone would for whom a close member of his family had been jailed for six months for pacifist statements, he had an inner understanding of the pacifist position. For Harrison Barrow, the man who had financed his education in England, and in whose house he had lived during school vacations, had gone to jail in 1918 for helping issue a pacifist leaflet. When my father wrote on pacifism in *The Forum* for June 1936 in a piece called "Pacifism: The Only Solution," he was being more of an optimist than a pacifist. In the statement "Peace must be prepared for as well as war, and you cannot prepare for both at the same time.", he may have been a realist. "As a soldier in the last war, I can testify that, at the moment when the choice has to be made, it is far less of an effort to follow the crowd into uniform than to stand out against it." He wrote of pacifism as a personal faith, a religion of the individual conscience. Armies were a sign of fear, not of courage. War psychology increases with every battleship and with every bombing plane. That war was an evil needed not to be argued. A month later, he published in *The Forum* an article entitled "Pacifism and Human Nature." (July 1936) He examined the issue of pacifism from an intellectual point of view as one who is interested in the subject. He explored the nature of a total commitment to pacifism and concluded that pacifism "must have its emotional appeal also and its hold upon the individual conscience. It must be a religion as well as a philosophy." He never said he had that religion. Yet he used to talk about the importance of having both an emotional and an intellectual commitment to a cause. He claimed there were certain crimes which civilized man could not and would not commit...slow torture, burning alive and choking to death by poisoned fumes the weak and the defenceless, thousands of old people, children and babies. In October 1938, he urged that "the place to beat Fascism was at home, not abroad, and the prior reason why we should not go to war in Europe is that we have a more urgent and constructive duty to perform at home." By 1941, George did refer to himself as a pacifist in an article in the *United Church Observer*, but this was not a long-term commitment, as was his commitment to socialism. The historian of Canada Ken McNaught thought George's socialism endured due to this emotional commitment. George was a social reformer. He may even at certain times have wished he were a pacifist like Harrison Barrow, but in his heart, he was too much a pragmatist and a man of his time. He may have been a pacifist up to a point during the mid-nineteen thirties, but he would never have gone to jail for the pacifist cause. He always had Harrison Barrow who went to jail for six months for his pacifism as the example of a true pacifist. In comparison, George did not consider himself one. On the other hand if he were alive today, he would certainly be working towards peace, and might be a pacifist. And one would certainly be left in no doubt about his position.

George's forthright manner in writing was even more apparent in his speaking. According to Margaret Lazaros who knew him first when she was a student in 1929-1930, and then as a political colleague, if my father was annoyed, everyone knew it. He had a tendency to storm from the room in the heat of the battle. On the other hand, he himself never bore a personal grudge. When other people took his anger personally, he was surprised. In writing to David Lewis, who in the early 1940s was CCF National Secretary and later became National President of the New Democratic Party, my father worried about this trait of his. In a letter to Lewis dated August 30, 1942, he expressed the fear that "there must be something in my manner that tends to make people think I am attacking them personally." He was referring to disagreements at the federal convention. During the period between 1937 and 1941 when he was managing editor of *The Forum*, he said that he was always having "quarrels" with one editor after another, and when on the CCF provincial Executive, he "was represented as having a knife into this person or that." He hoped that David Lewis did not feel that. We in his family knew that he was much more interested in the issue being debated than in attacking someone. No one took fewer personal swipes at anyone than he did. He was rarely, if ever, personally vindictive.

He could cause others to walk out in the storm of debate also, even in academic circles. The very polite Robert Getty, Head of the

Classics Department at University College in the 1950s, enjoyed inviting my parents to dinner. To some of these, I, too, was invited. This courteous and urbane man had invited a conservative British Classicist to his home. When the visitor started blaming trade unions for all Britain's woes, my father disagreed with him in a very reasonable manner. Suddenly, the man threw down his napkin and stormed from the house.

That George never bore a personal grudge was a wonderful quality in the head of a family. As he never pretended that he thought other than he did, it meant one always knew exactly where one stood with him. There was a complementary quality, the absence of any feeling that he had been mistreated. Since his loyalty was both with his mind and with his heart, no one doubted his loyalty to his politics, his academic institution, and to his family. In a crisis, he was very sensible and, in fact, more tactful with the members of his family than with his political colleagues. We often teased him about looking so fierce to the outside world, and told him he had the stern expression of the actor, Edward G. Robinson. Although he often remained quiet in social gatherings, he liked to entertain. My parents enjoyed inviting political and academic visitors to their house at the same time. We used to tell my father he could always get away from whoever was talking to him on the pretext of playing host, and that was why he liked his own parties.

Chapter 7: Some Students Who Became Friends

George did make lifelong friends with some of his students. One of the earliest, in 1929-30, was Margaret Sedgewick, who had the ambition of becoming a Classical archaeologist and whose brother later became prominent in the English department at the University of British Columbia. Among the courses she took for her M.A. was one with my father in Presocratic philosophy. She became an active socialist and political colleague and worked alongside my father on many a political campaign. When she married Morden Lazaros, who was a political organizer for the Ontario Federation of Labour, they were both loyal to my father throughout the years. Even in his old age they visited him frequently in my parents' apartment. Margaret showed him the regard that former students often have for their professors. When I asked her whether there wasn't some western Canadian resentment of an eastern Canadian professor's chairing political conventions, she claimed there was none whatsoever. Westerners were pleased, she said, to have someone of George's intellectual stature taking an interest in their political cause. What did annoy them, she continued, was that the CCF in Ontario was not doing better. Although it was the official opposition in the early '40s, western socialists thought that the CCF should have been the government. Margaret said westerners would have liked my father as he had a pleasant manner.

Natalie Hosford, who graduated from Trinity in Classics in 1941, had George in classes in which she was often the only student. She spoke of his great influence on her life, and the fact she devoted 35 years to the teaching of Classics. Although she had heard that he was demanding as a teacher, she was never in any way afraid of him, as students have told me they were because they were only in his larger classes. She said he was firm, strict and kind, and felt she would never have got through without his help. Several times she came to our house on Strathcona Avenue in the eastern Toronto Broadview riding where my father was a candidate. As a student, she said she was aware that the love of his life, aside from his family, was Greek. She took a graduate course in Euripides because he was giving it, and was delighted when he gave her the book he had written on the subject. When I interviewed her in 1992, she was a woman in her seventies, but was still devoting considerable time to volunteer work for her College. As a teacher she would emphasize to her students that only 19% of one's university education does one pay for and the rest the government pays. Her sense of community duty, if not directly due to my father's influence, was certainly one of which he would have been proud.

Another female student who was influenced by George was Jocelyn Rennie Hill. She kept up a correspondence with him for many years. When she was married and lived in England, she sent him pictures of her children. She thanks him for lending her money in 1969 and 1970. In 1980, when he was 81 and very depressed, she writes with affection how she owes everything to him:

> *First, starting me off right at Trinity, so that I always loved Classics and have always been glad to do it. Then getting me into Cambridge, so that I now have Cambridge as it*

> *were behind me....You supported me through all my difficulties and especially in '69, '70...[when he was responsible for] her "superb job" and her "emotional confidence."*

Another friend and former student of George's was Martin Ostwald, who was an undergraduate at University College, Toronto, from 1943 to 1947. Martin and several of his contemporaries worked for the CCF as students. Later, he became not so much a political colleague as an academic one. Martin retired in 1991 from a much respected career at Swarthmore College, a small college in a Philadelphia suburb. Like Trinity, it prides itself on its academic reputation. He said that as a student he was very aware of my father's political interests. Martin told me that at election time he had the job of putting up political posters. He took only one course from George, a post-graduate course in Plato, but they remained lifelong friends. As it happens, there was a physical resemblance between the two, and Martin acted the part of my father in a student skit. Coming in a bit late to his lecture, Martin firmly closed the window of his office and apologized for being late. George always closed windows, locked doors and closed curtains. A Classicist friend, Walter Donlan, remarked humorously to me at the 1991 American Philological Association meeting that Ostwald "did a very good Grube."

When my older sister Toni was ill during her third year at college, Martin said they felt the obligation as students to be kind to my father. When he was teaching a summer course at Columbia University, New York, without his family in 1948, Martin looked out for him, and was as hospitable as possible. They shared some very essential experiences. Both had left the European Continent as refugees. Martin had come as an interned German to Canada during the Second World War; George had fled as a Belgian refugee to England in 1914. Both he and Martin were Anglophiles. George spent his summer holidays before the war in England and sabbatical terms (the summer of 1960 and the spring of 1962) in Cambridge, England; Martin had had several sabbaticals in Oxford. Like my father, Martin's wife, Laure, owed her education to Birmingham Quakers. Both Martin and George were dedicated to their subject, the Classics, and both gave the impression that the Ancients provided direction and inspiration to their lives. Martin made his home in the United States. My father said that three countries, Belgium, England, and Canada, were enough for him. The very restrictions that Canada has compared to the United States worked in George's favour. Canada's fondness for things English, for example, was no problem to one who owed his educational opportunity to England. He was scrupulously polite when he was a visitor to an American university, but back in Canada, as he grew older, he got more and more the reputation for bluntness and saying exactly what he felt.

Not all the young students George made an impression on were in his classes. For some, there was the political connection. After his death, Mary Richardson Millard was instrumental in establishing an annual prize at Woodsworth College in the University of Toronto in memory of my father and two other socialists; the prize was to be awarded to the best student in a one-year diploma course for bilingual students seeking qualification as official translators. As the child of a socialist friend, Mary was invited to spend some time at our summer cottage at Muldrew Lake in Muskoka. She remembers George's driving her there when she was 13 or 14 and singing mostly sea-chanties all the way. When she was at college, and a member of the CCYM (Co-operative Commonwealth Youth Movement), the students were fearful of his arrival, only to find he was very jolly and even took part in the sports competitions. At the CCYM camp he proved to be quite an expert on the parallel bars. When Mary told my mother this story, she said she was not surprised since he had been a keen walker as a student in England. I remember his enjoying brisk walks with my mother along the Toronto Island boardwalk every evening.

Chapter 8: A Close Correspondence (1938 – 1954)

Another personal relationship that was very important to George was that with David Lewis. Their warm and cordial correspondence lasted from 1938 to 1954 and is in the National Archives in Ottawa. Each could express his respect and consideration for the other in a letter in a way that the telephone did not permit. When George ran as a candidate in the 1950 by-election in Broadview, David Lewis praised him to the chairman of the CCF nominating committee: "You will have a candidate of whom we are all proud." Lewis urged that the CCF campaign for the impending Broadview by-election be one of "the most enthusiastic we have ever waged." His election to the federal Parliament "would add a man of great courage, ability and integrity to the band of CCF fighters for the Canadian people." (Lewis letter, March 6, 1950)

With reciprocal respect, George showed understanding when David Lewis wished to resign as National Secretary. On July 11, 1949, he wrote of his admiration for Lewis's organizing ability during election campaigns and, indeed, at all times. The most the CCF had the right to ask was that David should hold off his resignation until the next convention, "though naturally, the longer the better." "I do hope it will be possible for you to remain national secretary for a while." He showed consideration for Lewis's position: "I know that you have been wanting to resign, and fully realize that you alone (with [Lewis's wife] Sophie) can make that decision." He felt that David's organizing ability was something he himself lacked. "I am personally not very useful in general campaigning," he wrote, but "I am some use in drafting things." (letter to David Lewis, April 21, 1948) Writing was what he had experience in, what he enjoyed and where he was successful. He put a great deal of energy into writing policy bulletins for candidates.

The two men discussed the close connection between *The Forum* and the CCF. One of the ideas in the creation of *The Forum* had been to reach a wider audience than the socialist circle. When George was an official of the Ontario CCF in 1944, he wrote a letter to David Lewis on June 13 in which he offered to remove his name from the masthead of *The Forum*. He felt he should not retain both positions, as his politics were too well known and that fact might decrease the impartiality and therefore the circulation of the magazine. Both were concerned not to provoke their readers. George wrote to David about two writers who wanted to do just that, to provoke *The Forum* readers, and wondered how he should deal with them. David suggested that the two be made to rewrite their sentences with objectivity. George conveyed this message to them.

Some of the letters are about the formation of a youth group. A few students at the University of Toronto were eager to revive that left-wing intellectual discussion group of the '30s and '40s, the League for Social Reconstruction. George mentioned David Corbett, a University of Toronto student, as a capable person who was keen on the idea. He wrote that *The Forum* needed the input of young people and that students should be encouraged to submit articles. Some students in Montréal were enthusiastic about the idea, too. George sounded delighted with this postwar group of young socialists. David Lewis suggested George be the CCF representative to work on the joint CCF and CCYM (Co-operative Commonwealth Youth Movement) Committee.

In 1950, George thought Trinity College might not approve of his running as a CCF candidate. He wrote to Lewis that he felt it was necessary to make up his mind quickly if he was to be a candidate so, "if there should be a row, I should probably give them the chance to change their mind again." (Feb. 12, 1950) In spite of this difference between his traditional college and his left-wing politics, he never complained about his college. They had stood behind him in 1939, and George never forgot that. He had devoted himself to the institution -- it was his life -- and it would have hurt him to leave, if he had won in the 1950 election. He admitted as much to the *Toronto Star* reporter who was writing a pre-election article on him. However, he continued, "You don't build things except by taking some risks."

In the 1950 by-election he was defeated, and he turned a corner. He decided the moment had come to devote his main energies in his 50s to scholarship if he was to become an international figure in the Classics field. He told Ken Bryden, a CCF organizer: "I'm getting stale. I've heard all this before. It's time to retire. I want to prove I can 'do it'." He more than proved he could to Classics specialists. At 50, he stopped trying to be a member of Parliament and began a decade of hard-working scholarship. However, that did not mean that he stayed completely out of political controversies. Some of the members of Woodsworth House in Toronto wanted to make money during a seller's market in the early fifties by selling this memorial of the CCF founder, J. S. Woodsworth: Frank Underhill and the Morrises who ran *The Forum* from the basement and lived in the coach house of this splendid old brick Jarvis Street house and paid only a nominal rent of $25 a month. My mother put some sharp words in a letter to Underhill in the 1952 controversy over the sale of

Woodsworth House: "It would be a pity if you were to be lost to the socialist cause." (March 30, 1953) In fact, her prediction proved true, as Underhill went over to the Liberals and became the curator of Laurier House in Ottawa. Just as vehemently, my father wrote to Underhill from Cambridge on April 25, 1952. He accused him of having faulty facts about an Executive change, the relationship between the party and the unions, and of not trying to see both sides of the Woodsworth House controversy:

> *I have difficulty recognizing myself, or any of my political colleagues in the horrifying picture of the power-drunk bureaucrats whom you so vividly, and so arrogantly, despise. (Underhill papers, Public Archives, Ottawa)*

Chapter 9: Range of Scholarly Writings

For his scholarly writings, George chose subjects in which he had a keen interest. One popular talk that Classical Associations asked him to deliver on several occasions was titled "Why study the Classics in this modern, busy, world?" (*University of Toronto Quarterly*, vol. 19, 1949-50, pp. 81-92) In 1960, he gave this as a lecture to the Ontario Classical Association to inspire the teachers who were fighting against great odds to keep Classics alive in the schools despite unsympathetic administrators. In his essay, he argued that the study of ancient Greece and Rome does equip a person to take part in the modern world. He listed all the qualities that such an individual should possess, and showed how the Classics could give you these. By studying Latin and Greek, one could acquire the capacity to use one's own language clearly and effectively. Because one had a more concise knowledge of the exact meanings and roots of words, it was easier to go on to the study of several modern languages. If one knew the ancient origins, one could acquire certain modern languages on one's own. Through the detachment that one acquires by studying the Classical civilizations, one can acquire the ability to think clearly without being blinded by prejudice and emotion. To balance this detachment was the commitment in ancient times to citizenship, to being an active member of one's community, to possessing a social conscience. For this, Athens was a good model because it attained a delicate and almost perfect balance between the individual and the state. Finally, he argued that the reading of so many masterpieces provided a standard of judgment by which one both enjoyed leisure and used it creatively.

George used his leisure time to translate the ancient masterpieces. For example, he translated Aristotle's *Poetics* (*The Art of Poetry*) with no idea of publishing it but for his own enjoyment. When I was at college, struggling through one of the available translations of this work, he suggested I might find the translation he had done easier to understand. He had written it for his own amusement, and put it away in a desk drawer. Only after I told him that I found it very clear did he think of publishing it. In "Why study the Classics in this modern, busy world?," George emphasized the length of time that Classics was in the forefront of our civilization in the western world. Our century is only an infinitesimal amount of time compared to the period when Latin and Greek were the only major European languages. "For twenty-five centuries Greek and Latin were the universal languages of Western culture." How lacking in humility was our culture to think it had no time for so much of our past! In this article, George blames school principals and school authorities for discouraging the study of Latin and Greek. He often told the story of Jarvis Collegiate in downtown Toronto where all of us children went. Many of the parents of these students were and still are immigrants. They know that what they want for their children is a traditional education. Through successive waves of immigration the school has remained academic for this very reason. The multiculturalism of the school is celebrated, rather than having all the children fit into some (often idealized) Anglo-Saxon mould. To challenge the mind is the school's first duty. It gives many immigrants their start in life.

George did criticize the school for its lack of interest in the whole development of the pupil. No doubt thinking of the interest he had himself developed as a pupil in drama and debating, he wrote the principal on the occasion of the cancellation of a play my sister was in:

> *Jarvis has a good reputation for scholarship but other schools are forging ahead in other ways as well. The students at Jarvis have no Debating Society, no Girls' Club, no Hi-Y for lower forms, no Open House Night in Education Week, above all no Student Council...a little training for democratic citizenship, in short.*

In his own life, he never just followed scholarship to the exclusion of all else. In his own terms, he was something of a Renaissance man with many interests. The article as to why we should study the Classics continues: Who is our modern hero? In concept it is still the Homeric man, the Odysseus who overcomes many obstacles before reaching his goal. "The Homeric hero [my father writes] is still, for better or for worse, embedded in the make-up of Western man generally." Yet the Greeks kept their minds invigorated by means of the poetry of Homer, a poetry itself "both very great and ever fresh," for Homer was the core of their education. Music and poetry were an integral part of the education of the hero. In fifth-century Greece "mathematics, astronomy, medicine, biology, logic, and the natural sciences were all established by men for whom poetry and music, together with athletics, made up the essence of their education." Later there was the exciting hero, Alexander the Great, who was responsible for the spread of Greek culture over Asia, making Greek "the common language of the Middle East." He pointed out that the Roman legacy to us was the practical organization of its empire. As the Greek was the man of culture, the Roman was "the man of action, the organizer, the extrovert." "Rome gave us more oratory, the organization of the great empire, the imperial roads along which travelled not only the legions but language and culture as well, and the development of the law." In conclusion, my father emphasized that it was to Greece and Rome that we must look for offering "the only way to retain any living contact with the greater part -- nearly five-sixths -- of our Western history."

All that George thought important on education and the art of rhetoric is reflected in his article on Cicero in *Phoenix* vol. 16, 1962, pp. 234-257. According to Cicero, the good speaker had to feel strongly about the subject matter on which he was addressing his audience. George spoke and wrote about matters about which he felt strongly. And there were a number of such matters. Anathema to Cicero and also to him was to know the correct style of public speaking without having anything to say. Such empty rhetoric could in fact do injury to the listener. As George described the Ciceronian curriculum, one gathered he would have favoured it as a general program in education: philosophy (including logic, ethics and psychology); political science; history and law, with a stiff course in the art of speech in both Latin and Greek. According to the Roman rhetorician Quintilian, the teacher must be lenient with a certain extravagance of imagination in some pupils, but this did not extend to watering down the curriculum. George did not consider the study of English literature a real academic discipline. He used to state in the Trinity Common Room that he was annoyed at people who came to University on Classics scholarships, and then went on to study English Language and Literature. The Trinity professors of English told me they enjoyed the irony of the fact that I did just that.

Cicero claimed that in order to be an excellent orator one must acquire knowledge of most things. This is in fact what was expected from the students at Cambridge University when George was a student there. They were to know their whole subject thoroughly. There was no time to work for a wage during the university holidays, as one was always reading more in one's subject. One could be asked anything at all in the Classics on one's final exam. George never understood the North American idea of working for the experience as well as money during one's college vacation. According to Cicero, the orator must shape his discourse both by selecting the right words and arranging them effectively. With George's keen interest in public speaking, he was no doubt paying particular attention to Cicero's words, selecting what he thought was useful. A good orator, according to Cicero, "must have a thorough knowledge of emotions with which nature has endowed man because the power and purpose of eloquence depend entirely on his capacity to calm or to excite the minds of the listeners." George had a great interest in oratory. Because my father and mother had met many kinds of human beings with varying levels of education through their political activity in the CCF, they felt they had gained a much more thorough knowledge of human nature in general.

In a lecture "What should we expect in education?," he defines four objectives, saying the emphasis varies at various times:

1. The training of emotions and 'character' is the most important at the lowest age level, at nursery school age.
2. The teaching of the necessary techniques, for example, elementary knowledge of reading, writing, arithmetic and logical thinking; roughly, the public school stage.
3. The training for a job; utilitarian knowledge such as vocational guidance.
4. The training of mind and body to develop the full personality.

Only 2 and 4 can ever be said to be completed.

George's office was in a tower, but in no sense an ivory one, according to Sandy McKay, a noted Classicist at McMaster University. In the mid-forties, a climb up the three flights of stairs to the Classics offices at Trinity meant to Sandy, then a pupil, an entry into an exciting world. There he had classes with Mary White, a lively ancient historian, or the urbane and courteous Sinclair Adams, or George Grube, outspoken member of the Co-operative Commonwealth Federation. They were all people whose Classical education had taught them to be active members of their community.

Like Cicero, George stressed that sincerity was a necessary component of public speaking. Cicero emphasized in particular the importance of rhythm in speaking: "I have often seen the crowd exclaim when the words fell into a balanced rhythm." Speaking and rhythm were interdependent. On the occasion of my taking a noon-hour class in public speaking while at University, Prof. Gilbert Bagnani of the University College Classics department told us to listen to Prof. Grube's lectures as a good example of cadence and rhythm. One of George's own models for prose was Winston Churchill. He collected his complete works and would read and re-read them, and he chose selections from them for his students to translate into Greek.

Another of Cicero's beliefs with which George felt himself in sympathy was the interdependence of one aspect of study on another. He subscribed to Cicero's view that any attempt to divorce literature from life, rhetoric from literature, politics from rhetoric, any of these from philosophy and education would be a grave error. One of the great values of studying the Classics was that a relationship existed in each of these pairs. The social sciences George objected to as he thought they worked in isolation from literature, politics and philosophy. When sociologists and psychologists quoted Homer without ever having read a word of either of his epic poems, he objected strongly. Also guilty of oversimplification of the Classical authors were English professors, or other academics in different fields. One of the standards that made the University of Toronto a great University was a course in Classical Literature that the experts, the Classics professors themselves, gave to students of English literature. In contrast were the Great Books Clubs which George blamed for not listening first to what a Classicist would have said before discussing the Classical authors.

When he became president of the Classical Association of Canada, he took the opportunity to visit universities in the Maritimes in early December, 1964. He lectured at the University of New Brunswick, Mount Allison, Dalhousie, and Saint Francis Xavier, and included an address to the Humanities Association of Fredericton. Just as when he had been president of the Ontario CCF 20 years earlier, he thought it important to keep in touch with as many of the local clubs as possible. One of his lectures was on the "Greek Idea of a Gentleman." He had to be both beautiful and good, and the sort of man known for honesty and trustworthiness. Truthfulness was important, along with average goodness and decency. He should be ready to undertake all the duties of a citizen. Physical beauty was an avowed aim for all, as was the development of the whole personality. No one part was to be developed at the expense of the rest. The Athenians were a race of brilliant amateurs and their motto was: Nothing too much. They weren't very interested in making money; a man should be free to enjoy the sunshine and the conversation of his fellows. The teachers of rhetoric, the so-called "Sophists," were travelling professors whom they admired but had no desire to imitate. A gentleman had to be moderately well off and able to discriminate in poetry, music, drama, and the fine arts. He should cultivate his natural power of speech or expression, and be friendly and easygoing. He should be critical of himself and others. Devoted to his country, he should be ready to give up his time, his money, and, if need be, his life in its service. He should be without a trace of cruelty. He should be a philosopher, athlete, and possess an Attic wit.

Another of George's favourite lectures was advice to the philosopher who wanted to take part in politics. He had the following advice for any philosopher who plunged into political life: go in quietly and unobtrusively, and, if you are willing to serve, you will soon find yourself leading due to your command of words. You will be careful never to use any word, phrase, or part of a sentence which, taken out of context, could be misrepresented to mean something which you did not say. He emphasized that co-operative thinking was difficult for the intellectual who was impatient with those less fluent in expressing ideas. Political ideas, however, must take into account the emotional or irrational, since these elements, too, were included in the varied experience of people from all different backgrounds. The philosopher's training in the power of expression is needed to put these ideas across in clear and simple language understood by everyone. A professor "should from time to time have to address audiences who express their feelings in no uncertain manner and do not hesitate to do so." He will be reaching toward that fuller development that Plato hinted at. As a candidate, he will never "be a 'good politician' and probably not want to be. Also, he is shy." To have to meet as many people as possible, and remember as many names as possible, was a waste for one trained to handle ideas. George spoke from the heart in this way about the difficulties he had encountered without dwelling on them in a personal or embarrassing way. His own academic career and college had been his life and very necessary to his peace of mind. He enjoyed the variety of people he had encountered in politics but his job as a professor of Classics was the breath of life to him.

Chapter 10: Homes and the Family

In the period when George was very involved in politics and when he was three times a federal candidate in the 1940s, he spent quite a bit of time away from home. But when he got older, he was around the house a great deal more. This was partly because we moved in 1948 from the East End of Toronto, where we had settled so that he could be in the riding in which he was a candidate, to an old Victorian row house at 5 Washington Avenue within ten minutes' walk from his office at Trinity College. I always presumed we had moved so that he could have lunch and supper at home, and then go back to his office. In fact, according to my mother, the main reason for our move was that my sister had been ill as a third-year college student. Moving closer to the university meant she could come back home for a rest whenever she felt like it. The downtown house, dark and old, was at first a shock to me. Because my father had a horror of going into debt -- he had been poor in his youth -- he refused to take on a heavy mortgage. From 1928 to 1943, the family lived in rented accommodation. One of these, 44 Farnham Avenue, where we lived from 1935 to 1936, was so large that my father was able to hold a dance with a 3-piece band for 100 people. The rent of $60 a month for this large house on Farnham was considered expensive, so we moved to a smaller house on the same street. From 1936 to

1940 we lived at 143 Farnham Avenue at $50 a month. Presumably the $10 difference was a big saving in those days, as well as the difference in the cost of heating a smaller house. Even so, No. 143 had four large bedrooms with screened-in porches off the back as well. My brother's third-floor bedroom was formerly the maid's quarters. My parents always said that our family as an academic one did not do too badly in the Depression since a professor had an assured salary.

As well as the occasion for a move, my coming into the world in 1935 seems to have brought many letters of congratulation from the Belgian relatives. They looked on my birth as a joyous opportunity for my parents to become closer. There is a letter from Aunt Lucie who was known for never writing, one from my father's cousin, Mimi, one from my father's Uncle Charles, and Aunt "Gusta." In fact, I must have been a great worry to my mother, as I was only three pounds at birth and had to be kept in the hospital an extra three weeks while she, an avid believer in breast-feeding, had to go down to the Toronto General Hospital to feed me.

Our next house, at 33 and 1/2 Thorncliffe Avenue, where we lived from 1940 to 1942, was a solid, bright and sunny 2-storey, 4-bedroom house with a huge terrace garden which my parents left to nature. It had two porches, one off the master bedroom and a lovely sunporch off the kitchen. There was plenty of room and many a Canadian CCFer stayed there, one of my favourite visitors being the charming Eugene Forsey. Later, my mother often regretted that she and my father had not bought this house, but my father was loath to go into debt. It was a happy house and I made school friends in the area that have remained faithful all my life.

The first house my family actually owned was at 37 Strathcona Avenue. It was bought for $3,200. We lived there from 1942 to 1948. It was a small and confining East End house with three tiny bedrooms. My sister and I had to share a room and we had to have our dining room table in the kitchen. My father came to the crowded kitchen meals less and less frequently; he began to remain at his college for dinner as well as for his customary lunch. From the moment we moved there, we felt like a family on alien turf. In spite of the British descent of the people, they were far removed from any knowledge of how matters really were in Britain. They had their own image of their fatherland. My parents kept up-to-date a correspondence with their many British friends and with the Barrows. It was a mean-spirited, grasping neighbourhood. Although I played with the children on the street, I could never trust them. One of their favourite games was stealing. The man next door had a supply of lumber which we stole, though what we could have possibly done with it, I can't imagine. The children taunted me as Jew-faced Jenny. Their relatives were fighting for the Jewish people, but they never saw further than that Canada was supporting some vague motherland, Britain. My sin in their eyes was that I was different from them: I liked to read books. Finally, my mother took me out of the neighbourhood school and I went to Moulton College, a beautiful old mansion at Yonge and Bloor headed by a Miss Trotter who pervaded the school with good sense and affection. For me the school was a haven of escape from the neighbourhood.

In the summers of the late nineteen-thirties and early forties, my mother took us children to Muskoka to escape the Toronto heat. The fear of polio in the large city of Toronto was such that my mother rented cottages in northern Ontario to escape contact with the disease. These cottages were wooden with rooms separated by partitions that did not reach the ceilings, an arrangement that gave little privacy. My father did not enjoy these summer holidays. He came for only a week or ten days each summer that we spent there. He would play the card game of Patience and pace the floor very impatiently.

Number 5 Washington Avenue, near the University, the next house we owned, was bought in 1948 for $7,500. It was a big, ugly Victorian semi-detached three-storey. My mother's legacy of 284.29 pounds from her mother, whose money was divided among her five children, helped with the purchase. The fact that the previous owner had died in one of the bedrooms was not lost on my brother and me; it was perfect for a haunted house. When I was at college, I tried to cheer up my third-floor study with bright pink walls, but the effect was still grim and grey. However, the house was so convenient for us all that we soon got used to its lack of beauty. Being near to the centre of the city and within walking distance of the University of Toronto was a great privilege.

In contrast to the dark University area shaded by its Victorian structures was the brightness of our Ward's Island summer cottage, which my mother and father bought in the fall of 1946, after a particularly gruelling hot summer that my father had endured in the city. That September he vacationed for a week at the Centre Island summer home of the Cork sisters, two socialists who rented rooms to vacationers. My father loved the way one could walk along the boardwalk and look out at the glistening water and distant horizon. My parents bought at first sight the cottage at 76 Lakeshore Avenue, Wards Island. Right from the beginning, it was a mecca for our friends who wanted to escape the oppressive heat of a Toronto summer. Every Sunday afternoon, my parents had open house welcoming at least half-a-dozen people and often more than a dozen showed up. Visitors would bring their swimsuits to brave the frigid waters of Lake Ontario. My mother would buy two large slabs of cake, one chocolate and one white, to serve with tea for whoever showed up. Different sorts of people would arrive: august academics would find themselves taking tea with socialist welders.

For the first few years that we had the Island home, we eagerly looked forward to spending May to October there, although there was no central heating, hot water or refrigeration. Somehow the house seemed more of an adventure to us children without these amenities. No cars were allowed on the Island. As a result, the air was very clean. The large, bright, two-storey, four-bedroom cottage faced the lakeshore. There was a delightful boardwalk where one could always count on a friendly greeting from neighbours strolling along -- unless of course they were running to catch a boat. Seeing successful downtown Toronto businessmen breathlessly running to catch the boat somehow added to the friendly atmosphere. It was only a ten-minute boatride to downtown Toronto. Not that all the Island people were from the same social stratum; far from it. There was a healthy mixture of all sorts of people, depending on the size and therefore expense of the house. How enjoyable it was to go part way to school or work by boat. As before, I was sure that my parents had bought the Island home for the convenience of my father. In fact, we all benefitted from the cottage's beautiful setting and the fact that city friends dropped in regularly.

Since it was a cottage, it fell to us children to do whatever repainting was required, and a visiting friend might be co-opted to help paint the dining room. This made the house even more our own and we could always go for a swim afterwards. The furniture was of the wicker sort that had a faded elegance. Elegant too was a huge grand piano belonging to a previous tenant, and some of the tables, which would have been considered valuable antiques today. My father had chosen well.

Years later, people would often tell me how much they enjoyed visiting our cottage. Visitors from abroad would plan their stay to coincide with our time there. Harrison Barrow from Birmingham, England, came, flying in an aeroplane for the first time in his life at the age of 79. Aunt Lucie from Antwerp, Belgium, stayed there. Marion Billson, a Cambridge fellow student of my mother's, came.

The Island visitors' book tells a story in itself of the variety of people who visited. There were politicians like, for example, True Davidson, city councillor, and politicians-in-the-making, like 17-year-old Stephen Lewis. There were groups of youth: a Jarvis Collegiate Grade 13 September party and the Unitarian Church young peoples' group. Trinity College Classicists came: Mary White and Des Conacher and his wife, Mary. We also played host to the successful farming family, the Bicks, originally professionals to whom Canada offered refugee-status during World War Two provided they tilled the land. There was my sister's wedding party of September 7, 1954 with everybody from the cleaning lady, Lilla Petrucci, who had been with us for as long as anybody could remember, to George's former student, now Anglican minister, Graham Cotter, to the Latin poetry specialist, Robert Getty, to my sister's Quaker co-religionists, Roy and Margaret Smith. The Canadian writer James Reaney and his wife paid us a visit on June 23, 1957.

George arranged CCF council meetings there. People felt free to pay a casual visit on a summer Sunday. The extent of the hospitality was quite phenomenal. The summer of 1962 was particularly busy. The Grubes had the CCF Spadina riding to a picnic on July 8 and at least 60 people came. My wedding reception with 100 guests was held there on July 28. On August 18 there was an NDP council meeting for 40 people. Aside from these events there was the usual stream of summer visitors both casual and those invited by both adults and children. Rarely would we children have friends to stay in the city house, for we thought it might disturb my father if he wanted to write. There, the hierarchy was very clear. We never presumed that matters should be otherwise. But at the Island home, we had a lot of freedom. In high school, I had class parties here which my mother would chaperone while my father stayed in the city house.

The day-to-day business of raising children my father left to my mother with the result that we thought of consulting my father only in a crisis. Not once did he ask the typical father-at-the-dinner-table question: "How was school to-day?" Moreover, he showed no interest or concern in what we were doing at school. As a result, each of us worked like the devil at our school work to try to get his attention. Even though we weren't sure it made much difference to him, we thought he was probably pleased if we did well. My brother and I won several scholarships from high school to university, but my father never came to any of our graduations. Nor would we have expected him to.

I do remember his reacting to one thing I told him about my school work. He himself had written a 306-page book on Plato. When I reported to him that our Grade 11 ancient history examination asked us to tell all we knew about Plato in not more than one paragraph, he was very amused. Since my father kept his distance on ordinary matters, we did not question his judgment on important decisions. When he decided something was best, it was very difficult to oppose him.

These days young people frequently take a year off between high school and university, but in the early 1950s when my brother John wanted to, it was relatively rare. By the time John had finished high school, since he was gifted in picking up modern languages, he spoke French fluently and Spanish rather well. Probably John should have continued to travel and work for a year or so to develop this skill. Yet, my father opposed his wish. To be fair to my father, since John would have had to forgo hundreds of dollars of scholarship money, it was an important decision with good reasons on both sides. I can still remember listening, or not being able to help listening, as the loud argument went on between the two of them. John continued on the traditional road of going directly to college, though within the first few months he switched from Classics to Mathematics, Physics, and Chemistry, and then to Oriental languages. In my own case, after one year at Trinity College which I found different from the multicultural downtown high school I had attended, I wanted to change to University College. Since my father thought it would be showing disloyalty to his employer and might possibly embarrass him, he insisted on my staying at Trinity. It never occurred to me to insist on the change against his wishes.

Since my father didn't involve himself in routine matters, my mother had to bear all the frustrations, the annoyances, hear our complaints and put up with the dislike which teenagers project on whoever of their family is around. I believe I was always in a bad mood at breakfast, for example, but instead of my father having breakfast with us, he had it on a tray in his room. With his habit of reading until the small hours of the morning, he did not like to get up early and never lectured before 10:00 a.m.

Besides his enthusiasm for the rhetorical style of Winston Churchill already mentioned in chapter 9, George was fond of the works of George Bernard Shaw and in particular admired his trenchancy and wit. George enjoyed Shaw's irreverance in the following passage, which he once set as a piece to be translated into Greek:

> *As the great champion of freedom and national independence, he (the Englishman) conquers and annexes half the world and calls it colonisation. When he wants a new market for his adulterated Manchester goods, he sends a missionary to teach the natives the Gospel of Peace.*

George emphasized the music of words and literature. From Homer on down, literature was meant to be heard. One can find his emphasis on the rhythm of words in his articles on Homer, on

Euripides, and in all his comments on public speaking. His "Remarks on the Greek and Roman Critics," an address on December 30, 1965 at the Convention of the Speech Association of America, emphasizes this point. Even in his everyday speaking, there was a rhythm to my father's words.

In spite of the distance my father kept, there was a great deal of affection in our family. My sister and I always kissed my father and mother goodbye, and my father always greeted my mother with a kiss when he came home. Probably this was because of our Continental origins; many Canadians, I noticed, did not greet members of their family this way.

What children consider harmless teasing of each other at the dinner-table can certainly sound like bickering to a father, and my father was no exception. Like most adolescents, we would be surprised that anyone could find our interesting repartee annoying. My father's general expression at the dinner table was one of resignation. When we brought guests home to dinner (which we frequently did), his expression did not change. In general my friends weathered this situation rather well. One of my college friends, Sira Beaumayne, told me years later how much she enjoyed his grim, jowelled expression.

My friends who had known my father since their childhood and were genuinely fond of him remembered how he used to exaggerate his expression of distaste when he had to take some medicine at the table. One of them, Joyce Wallace, would giggle delightedly when he made a dreadful face. Many people concluded -- perhaps too hastily -- that he disapproved heartily of what they were saying. His expression was partly put on intentionally. No doubt it was a useful defence at the innumerable meetings he attended both at university and politically. Partly his facial expression was a result of the fact he worked very hard all his life. Two of his former students, Caroline

Williams and Paul Burns, both now in Vancouver, told me how terrified they were when they first met him. He had reached the pinnacle of his profession in Canada relatively early, at the age of 32.

My parents often spoke of retiring to the Island house. But in 1968 the city which owned the land decided to expropriate the Island houses in order to make a large city park which would be more accessible to everyone. Only the less expensive houses were allowed to stay, as the inhabitants argued they would never be able to afford equivalent houses in the city. Down came the fine elegant villas and left were the ragtale village cottages. Although regretful, my father with his usual practicality accepted the inevitable.

The $7,500 the city gave them for the Island house contributed to my parents' purchase of an apartment in Rosedale at 158 Crescent Road for $24,500. In 1968, they also sold their Washington Avenue house for $31,000. Clearing out both houses was a great chore, but, as usual in a crisis situation, my father did a great deal of the work. The one item he could never bring himself to throw or give away were the books. Books were too human for him to be able to dispose of them.

The Rosedale apartment had to be made to include as many books as possible. There was a large study, but the hall was diminished into a narrow corridor in order to make room for large bookshelves. As for Toronto real estate, they had indeed gone from rags to riches, from an ugly duplex on Howland Avenue to Rosedale. The apartment was a co-op, which kept it within their socialist principles. There was a living room large by apartment standards so that they were still able to entertain. Professors and socialists still rubbed elbows at many a Grube party.

His position as Head of Department in a privileged, private college allowed him a certain freedom. Yet his way of thinking ran counter to his working environment, which was a conservative, high Anglican college. A Trinity academic's daughter, Jane Barker, told me how her father, Arthur Barker, the Miltonist, emphasized that my father was "both a socialist and an agnostic," as if one of these heresies was not enough. A difficulty for George was that his training in Cambridge, England, was foreign to the type of teaching the Classics professors were doing at the University of Toronto when he arrived. George and Gilbert Norwood, Head of Classics at University College who had also come over from Britain, both wanted to write and teach to the average college reader. In an interview with Robin Harris, who was gathering material for a work on the University of Toronto and who later became principal of the Ontario Institute on Studies in Education (*University of Toronto Archives*, Nov. 1973), George hints at a certain narrowness among the other Classicists who were following the old way. Although he praises the good training they gave and their insistence on reading the great authors in the original, they were not, in his opinion, attempting to reach an international audience in their ideas or their writing. In contrast, he calls himself and Norwood the first of the modern Classicists who aimed at a larger audience. At a meal at Hart House, the university's principal social and cultural gathering place, George would seek out Norwood's table to enjoy his conversation. These two scholars' efforts led within the University to the introduction of courses in translation. Harris in the above-mentioned interview states that when he came to Trinity as a student in 1937, he was conscious of two scholars of international repute: my father and G. Wilson Knight.

In spite of the fact George attained international recognition, his own university never gave him an honorary degree. This did bother him. He felt the provost of Trinity at the time, Derwin Owen, a former student in fact, couldn't bestir himself to recommend such a controversial figure for the honour. George with disapproving irony would quote Owen as saying: "If you don't know what to do, the best thing to do is nothing." Owen's philosophy of life was in direct contradiction to George's. He could not bear to do nothing. His political activity in the Tory city that Toronto was in the '40s, '50s, '60s and '70s counted against him. His politics worked in his favour when he received an honorary degree from the University of Victoria, B.C. on May 26, 1973, at a time when the New Democrats were the provincial government. His contribution to the CCF was listed among his achievements.

In Toronto, there were at that time few honorary degrees given to those not Canadian or British born. He had left England hoping to escape such narrowness, but he had not escaped it. In spite of limited horizons on the part of his superiors, he decided to remain in his Canadian job, although, as already mentioned, distinguished offers came from the United States and England. He used to say that three countries were enough. My father's early youth had certainly been difficult. We know he had been orphaned at 12 and had been poor. How difficult it was was shown by the fact he never talked about it. His family spoke French, the language of the bourgeois in Antwerp at that time. How abrupt the change at 15 to a strict Quaker British couple's care must have been! Then, in his twenties, he had to fit in at Cambridge, Kent, London, Swansea, and Toronto, all very different settings.

How far did politics really play the front runner in George's interest? Often those who came to him found him abstracted. When John Cole first began teaching Classics at Trinity in 1949, he asked George how he should approach his courses. George replied, "Do what you like." A couple of days before meeting his first class, John went to him again for more specific instructions, and got the same answer. George dismissed him in his usual fashion: by taking up a book and beginning to read. Those under him had complete freedom to teach their courses the way they wanted. Was this due to a belief in freedom or to lack of interest? When he did take an interest, there was no doubt about his opinion.

The same diffidence could be found in other matters. Students might find him taking them through the text of a Classical author as his sole approach to that author. To read the text as most of his students were doing, slowly, would have to be done before getting to the stage of commenting on it. He had little use for those who were willing to comment on the text before having read it in the original.

Chapter 11: Closing Years

My father did not hold on to positions of power into his old age. In 1961, when he was 62, he chaired his last national convention under a gruelling August Ottawa sun at the changeover from the CCF to the New Democratic Party. The *Toronto Star* of August 1, 1961, read:

> *When a professor of Classics throws off his suit coat, puts on a green eye-shade and starts to light a filter-tip cigaret at the filter end in front of a crowd of hundreds, it can be assumed he's getting down to hard work.*

No doubt the turning point from the political movement of the CCF to the political party of the NDP seemed to him an opportune time to start thinking of making room for younger and more vigorous politicians. A few months later, he chaired a provincial convention in Niagara Falls, Ontario. He was a powerful chairman, but some of the young members like David Lewis's son Stephen were eager to have a go themselves. Stephen had had a great deal of success as a leader of the socialist mock parliament at the University of Toronto, winning a victory in the very conservative times of the late fifties, and impressing his audiences greatly with the vigour and rhythm of his oratory. He may have been subconsciously preparing for his later roles as NDP leader in Ontario and Canada's ambassador to the

United Nations. He later pushed aside Donald Macdonald, the Ontario party leader, to the disgust of many an old-timer. Both he and John Brewin were champing at the bit to get on with being politicians. John was one of those I heard criticize my father's chairing. My father was very generous with his time with students even though he didn't teach them. When John, as a student at Trinity, consulted my father about whether he should continue his studies in order to become a lawyer or go directly into politics full-time, my father advised continuing his professional training. With professional papers in hand, he pointed out, one would have more expertise to contribute to politics. What he himself had done was to be both professor and politician.

Having both a profession he liked and an active political life meant there were times that one passion held sway over the other. While reading a Classical work for review in the summer of 1946, my father decided if he was to make his name internationally in Classical scholarship, it was time to give up devoting all his spare time to active political work and devote this instead to scholarship full-time. He was to review for the *American Journal of Philology* a massive three-volume work, the English translation of Werner Jaeger's *Paideia*. Like every project he undertook, he did his preparation carefully, taking the whole summer to read around his subject. Here was a German scholar claiming that Greek expressions of personal emotion and thought had nothing subjective in them and George thought just the opposite. Jaeger did not see that a *sophos* [wise man] was a poet not a philosopher (*American Journal of Philology,* volume LXV11, p. 204). George was sure the Sophists' strength lay in the brilliant new system of education they invented. Imagine Jaeger's condemning Euripides as bourgeois and considering Aristophanes unimportant. Nor did Jaeger deal with the character and outlook of the Greek people themselves. George felt if he were going to do a better job of interpreting the Greeks, then he'd better do it. He was getting into his late forties. If he was going to make a name for himself, he had better start now.

There had been the gap of a decade when he had devoted most of his spare time to politics. If we look at his published works, it is difficult to find a 10-year lull in his academic career, but I suppose one could say it was from his mid-30s to his mid-40s. One reason for writing books was that he needed the money. In 1946, for the first time in years, he had a salary increase under the new provost of Trinity, Reginald Seeley. The maximum for a department head at Trinity was $4,500, and it would still be some years before he reached this amount. He knew he could write books, and would be able to reach a wider audience and sell more books than most Classicists. He felt his mission was to popularize the Classics. His first book had been an analysis of Plato, *Plato's Thought* (London, 1935, repr. 1958, 1970, 1980). He himself followed the stages of man's life as outlined by Plato, playing his part as elder and statesman at the appropriate time. Throughout his life, scholarship had afforded objectivity and release to his life of political action.

His books continued to be published: *The Drama of Euripides* (London, 1941, repr. 1961, 1973); *Longinus On Great Writing* (New York, 1957); *A Greek Critic: Demetrius on Style* (Toronto, 1961); *Marcus Aurelius, The Meditations* (Indianapolis, 1963); *The Greek and Roman Critics* (Toronto, 1965, paperback 1968). Throughout all this time, there were numerous articles and book reviews, some dating back to 1929, less than a year after his arrival in Canada.

American Classical scholars recognized fully his scholarly achievements. In 1952 the University of California at Berkeley invited him to join their Classics department. A former Canadian, Louis McKay, approached my father. He wanted him to replace a man who had lost his job due to political principle. The salary was excellent; he would never again have had to worry about money and his family would be well provided for. My brother John had just been hit by a terrible arthritis and I had university yet ahead of me. George could have just done his work which he liked and was good at. He decided to go to the president of the University of Toronto and tell him of his dilemma. The president called the provost of Trinity immediately and said "Don't let Grube go" and arranged for a raise in salary. The man George would have replaced was a European-born Classicist, Ludwig Edelstein, who had lost his Berkeley job for refusing to sign the loyalty oath which American universities were then insisting their teaching staffs adhere to. At the time, anti-intellectuals were hunting down academics and unjustly accusing them of being Communists. It was the McCarthy era in the United States. Joseph McCarthy, a U.S. senator from Wisconsin, had persuaded the authorities that Communism was rampant on university campuses and that many professors had been and were still members of the Communist party. His hearings were broadcast on TV and the media effectively increased the fear on both sides. All professors at Berkeley had to sign a document swearing a non-Communist oath. Edelstein had a European's intolerance for forcing professors to sign an oath limiting their academic freedom. He knew what the Nazis had done in Germany; of course, he refused to sign such an oath. George could not replace a man who was being fired for his political principles. He did say that he felt he would not have taken the stand Edelstein took. George was fundamentally a practical man. At the same time, he admired Edelstein for taking such a firm position. George told Berkeley why he could not accept a professorship there. Berkeley took it personally and, it seems, never forgave him.

My father had several other job offers and approaches in the 1950s. Bernard Knox on a train ride from the American Philological Association meetings, which were and still are always held in the snows of winter amid great transportation difficulties, asked him if he would be interested in heading up the Centre for Hellenic Studies in Washington which Harvard University had newly established. Johns Hopkins, then a university with a distinguished Classics tradition, invited him to accept one of their senior professorships in 1960. Professor G. Mandelbaum wanted him to come. He would have earned $16,000 a year, a lot more than he was making at Trinity. The political climate in the United States at that time did not appeal to my father. The universities had not recovered from the blow McCarthyism had dealt academic freedom. In an interview with Milton Eisenhower, the president of Johns Hopkins University, my father told the brother of the President of the United States that he felt he should make clear to him that he was active in social democratic politics in Canada. Milton Eisenhower replied clearly and with appealing understatement, "Don't worry. I have powerful connections." Within the family, my mother claimed they would never leave Canada and their friends, particularly their political ones. My father asserted that three countries were enough for him. On another occasion, the State University of New York at Buffalo even asked him to name his price, but how could one put a price label on my parents' reasons for staying in Canada?

Their short stays in the States they enjoyed enormously. In 1953, my father was the Walker Ames Professor at the University of Washington in Seattle for the spring term. He had difficulty entering the country because the original file from the smear campaign in 1944 which labeled him a Communist was available to the U.S. immigation authorities. The correction had never been made when the libel case was won. A lawyer had to be retained to change the data on my father's file. M. J. Coldwell wrote a statement in support of my father's character. In spite of the inauspicious beginning, my parents enjoyed their visit to the West Coast enormously. They returned with glowing reports about the weather, the sea, and the mountains. In 1959-1960 they both thoroughly enjoyed the community of scholars at the Institute for Advanced Sudy in Princeton, New Jersey, where my father was a Guggenheim Fellow for the academic year. In 1967 they spent the second semester at the University of Cincinnati where George had been invited to deliver the prestigious Semple Lectures. He chose as his topic "How did the Greeks look at Literature?" and they were well looked after by the Caskeys. John was Professor of Archaeology in charge of a dig on the Greek island of Kea, which my parents had visited and which my mother found particularly charming, and Betty (Gwyn) Caskey had been a Classics student at the University of Toronto. In 1968, after partial retirement, my father went as a visiting professor for one-half year at the University of North Carolina at Chapel Hill. There the George Kennedys, among others, received them with gracious hospitality. Americans treated my father with great respect, as I saw personally when he gave a lecture at Pennsylvania State University. Every single Classicist there was very welcoming. One in particular, Joe Cotter, even found time to engage my father in his favourite hobby, a game of chess.

Just as he left political chairing at the appropriate time, so he retired from departmental chairing at 65. He carried no malice towards his successor, and never indicated that matters had been better under his chairmanship. He was too busy with his own work to have time for such games that seem to be common in the university world. In spite of my father's objectivity, he had a few choice targets at which he directed his irony. As he became older, he claimed the younger generation of scholars had Ph.D.-itis; he himself had never thought of getting a Ph.D., but just got on with the business of doing his own scholarship, writing and publishing. In the Oxford-Cambridge system of his day, it was the undergraduate degree that counted. One paid for one's M.A. if one needed it. A scholar was not a dependent but went out into the adult world, writing as a mature person, without having to choose an obscure topic "to please some damn committee."

Another object of his irony was what he called "foot and note" disease. He objected to books and articles that were overburdened with footnotes. Again following the Cambridge direction of his day of appealing to a wider audience, he saw that the object of writing was to communicate what one had to say clearly and simply, and not to explain one-third of a page of writing with two-thirds of a page of footnotes. My father thought that the business of the scholar was to work directly from the author involved and not to show how many of the secondary sources he or she had read with an excess of footnotes.

As he got older, and it became more difficult for him to go to the University Library or his office, he worked at home, making a profitable business of his hobby of translating texts from Greek to English. The Bobbs-Merill Library of Liberal Arts in Indianapolis was delighted to publish them. An offshoot of this company, the Hackett Publishing Company, issued as their very first publication my father's translation of Plato's *Republic*. Frances and Bill Hackett ascribed their success as a business partially to the fact that one of their first publications was my father's book. The Hacketts became friends of my parents, and I remember my father's being delighted with the hospitality they received when they went down to Indianapolis and stayed in the publishers' home in 1975. Bill Hackett wrote my parents a charming Christmas card that year, in which he confided that their secret was that they looked on the Grubes as their spiritual but somewhat forbidding parents: "Don't you agree that a certain amount of awe should be mixed in with the love and respect due parents from faithful, loyal children? If that be the case, Fran and I as dutiful children send you a bit of all three."

In 1980, Hackett brought out a new edition of my father's translation of Plato's *Republic* with the help of Donald J. Zeyl for the revision. Hackett's own admiration shines through in the writing on the cover:

> *... one must have the mind to translate Plato.... Prof. Grube's peers have for many years recognized and awarded this quality. But in addition one must have something else...not truly definable...to translate a work of this kind. Perhaps it could be labelled 'character.' If character means integrity and discipline, experience, courage, G.M.A. Grube can be said to have brought all these qualities to this new translation of one of the world's oldest and greatest books.*

Hackett also published second editions of his translations of Plato's *Five Dialogues (Euthyphro, Apology, Crito, Meno, Phaedo*) in 1981, and *Trial & Death of Socrates* (*Euthyphro, Apology, Crito,* death-scene from *Phaedo*) in 1980, as well as *Phaedo* the same year. They reprinted his *Meditations of Marcus Aurelius* in 1983, and a second edition of his *Plato's Thought* in 1980. His publishers stood by him like loyal friends into his old age, and both even came to his memorial service in Toronto after his death in 1982.

The older he got the more marked was his tendency to save his charm for outsiders and to complain within the confines of the family. My mother let him indulge the aches and pains of old age and an appearance of being miserable in the family setting. On one occasion, when he was in his 70s, we all went with a family friend to the O'Keefe Centre in downtown Toronto to see the *Threepenny Opera*. For the first act, my father sat between my mother and me, looking very much as if he wished he were elsewhere. At intermission, an old student from the 1940s greeted him. As we took our seats again, my father sat next to the family friend and was as charming as could be.

In his 70s, he didn't really want to travel outside Canada much. In the spring of 1972, he went as a visiting professor to the University of Victoria, British Columbia. The Lieutenant Governor of British Columbia bestowed an honorary degree on him on May 26, 1973. In the citation is mentioned his invaluable counsels in establishing graduate studies in Classics. At the time, there was a New Democratic Party provincial government, and in the acclaim, his participation in politics was cited. It was a fitting tribute, though he himself still felt he had not yet accomplished enough in scholarship, in politics or in his family.

My father's awards seemed more than deserved. This was the point made when he received the "Goodwin Award of Merit" at the annual meetings of the American Philological Association (since renamed the Society for Classical Studies) in 1967 at Boston. This distinction is given annually to a Classical philologist.

In the spring of 1973, he came to Oxford, England, to visit our family when we were there on sabbatical leave. The Oxford academics were very pleased to meet him, but he felt a great deal of discomfort in travelling. Also, in August 1973 he contracted pneumonia after holidaying with some Classicist friends. Phil and Estelle Delacy were delighted to have my parents as guests at their home in Long Beach, New Jersey, while our family, the Podleckis, rented an apartment nearby. The weather was very hot and the humidity affected my father's lungs. He never had cut down on his smoking. He had to travel home stopping at his least favourite airport, Newark.

When my father was in his late 70s and early 80s and no longer able to visit us in Vancouver, I exchanged houses in the summers of 1978 and 1981 with people who lived near my parents' apartment in Rosedale. That way, my parents enjoyed their grandchildren without creating too much upset in their own lives. They did have visitors to stay in their three-bedroom apartment. Lucie, though older than George, was still able to travel. She had always been energetic. At the age of eighty, when she retired from the YWCA, though she was to go back part-time for several years, she was given a trip around the world. Of course, she stopped to see her brother in Toronto as she did me in Vancouver and her grandson in Japan. She had been widowed and so was travelling alone, interviewing directors at the different YWCAs. The Vancouver YWCA director treated her well and enjoyed a spirited discussion with her. At the Vancouver airport a male official was unwilling to let her on the plane early, and I had to persuade him she was over 65. She was to make the trip to visit George in his Rosedale apartment twice more. Her adventurous spirit a Belgian reporter had tried to capture a few years earlier:

> *Infatigable animatrice, depuis 52 ans elle est pour ses jeunes une amie sure, une confidante, un guide, un soutien et la lucidité de sa brillante intelligence lui permet sans crainte d'avoir pour eux parfois toute la tendresse d'une mère. Ses yeux bleus porcelaines sont enjoleurs quand il faut et chavirés de furieur quand la passion l'emporte. Si nous étions elle et moins d'enragées féministes, j'oserais dire: Quel homme, cette femme.*
>
> *An untiring director, for more than 52 years she has been for young people a sure friend, a confidante, a guide, a protector, and her clear, brilliant intelligence has been mingled with the warmth of a mother. Her porcelain blue eyes brighten when she is aroused by emotion. If we were her and less the angry feminists we are, I would dare to say, "What a man this woman is!"*

The energy and the flashing porcelain eyes were shared alike by George and Lucie. Similar to his sister in this respect, George remained faithful to his place of employment for more than 40 years.

In 1978, while my mother had a holiday with friends, my father stayed with us for a week. I had two of my old friends in to dinner. Joyce had been a friend of mine since kindergarten, her husband Bill since high school and he was now a top business executive. Bill was very upset because his workers were trying to organize a union. When my father and I were talking about it afterwards, he said simply "Well, he's management, you see." This seemed most unlike the Classicist who had verbally attacked my mother-in-law on the subject of unions at a dinner in our house in his early 70s. Was this just the mellowing of age, or was my father reacting to someone who had presented a point of view opposite to his own but in a genuine manner? I think it was the latter. If a person took the diametrically opposed viewpoint to my father's but had good reasons, then my father respected him.

My father did not seem to have time for regrets. According to my brother John, if my father had stayed in England he would have been elected as a Labour party member and probably been given a cabinet post in Atlee's post-World War Two Labour government. If my father had accepted the academic postings offered to him in the United States, he would have had more recognition as a Classicist and certainly more money. My father never expressed regrets; I think they didn't occur to him. Never did he give the impression he wished he were elsewhere, but gave his loyalty 100% to the work, scholarly or community, in which he was engaged. If he did have regrets, it was rather in himself. According to my mother, he had not achieved as much as he wanted to. Along the same lines, he never expressed verbally, in our presence anyway, any jealousy or envy of another. An occasional light irony was rather his trademark. Although he was very pleased to be named a member of the Royal Society of Canada in 1951, he remarked on the induction of not so academic a scholar, "It's not really worth so much after all, is it." Did ageing account for this irony? I think it was always part of his nature. His fellow Classicist and former student Martin Ostwald recalled saying, "Well, George, with all these 'How to...' books around, there must be one on 'How to stop smoking.' " My father replied, "I expect there is. I know, Martin. You read the book and then tell me what's in it."

My father never pretended to be interested in something if he wasn't. We, his family, used to tell him that the photographers at political conventions caught him rubbing his eyes in boredom or giving a wide yawn. If I brought friends home who did not interest him, he would continue to read in the same room. When, in retirement, my mother invited neighbours to the apartment in Rosedale, he would just 'tune out.' My mother used to say he was so afraid of being a garrulous old man that he didn't say anything at all.

Sometimes Belgians would want to meet him because of his having the same national origin. He did not feel this was enough of a reason to speak to someone. In Philadelphia, in 1965, at an international Classicists' meeting, a Belgian Classicist asked me to introduce him to my father. My father just said "How do you do?" and walked away. Later he told me he found it an awful bore when other Belgians wanted to meet him. At the same Classics conference in Philadelphia, I phoned our only known relative in North America, my mother's oldest brother. I was sure my father would accept with us an invitation to visit my uncle, but he said quite bluntly he'd rather not. It must have been a great saving of energy on his part not to feel one had to be polite to people if one didn't want to.

Certainly, he did not flatter in order to get anywhere. Simple terms of flattery that most consider everyday would not have passed his lips. His sister Lucie was the same. She was a straight talker, and for this reason people liked her at once. She was always willing to go more than halfway to talk to someone. Although my father could be charming, he was by nature much more reserved than she was. Such directness made both my father and his sister popular with my children, for Lucie and he would talk to them as if they were adults. For that the children loved them. My father did not 'pretend' with his grandchildren. When playing chess with his ten-year-old grandson, he did not just let him win. On the other hand, children were to respect the rights of their elders for quiet, etc. There was no doubt that they were to have regard for the hierarchy of age.

What his friends and family miss most after his death is the detachment with which he could view a problem and thereby enable one to come to a solution with his assistance, his reasonableness and at the same time his commitment. That the two could exist together in an individual was his distinction. There are examples of such reasonableness in his extant letters. As a young teacher in Ottawa, fed up with my job, I had written to him while he was spending his first sabbatical at the age of sixty as a Guggenheim scholar at the Princeton Institute for Advanced Study. It was the beginning of my second year of high school teaching, and I was unsure whether I wanted to continue with teaching as a career. My apartment-mate was in her first year of teaching and we were both thinking of getting another type of job. He wrote quoting my aunt by marriage, herself a teacher and a recent visitor at the Institute: "A good teacher always feels like quitting at least twice a year!" His letter continued with some of the few words of advice I ever received from him:

> *I expect you will find your natural level somewhere between the too strict and the too friendly, before long. Anyway, your Principal is evidently pleased, and however difficult or mistaken he may be, obviously has had enough experience to know a good teacher when he sees one. Anyway, there probably is no intelligent mature person who is not depressed quite often! At least until they get to sixty;*

> *then one just gives up trying to think what else one is going to do in life. However, we all enjoy life too.*

As I read this now, I can see how sound his advice was. He actually did not advise me to give up teaching, although he himself had impetuously done so at the high-school level. For one thing, he would not have wanted to lose his financial investment, for, on the whole, his investments did very well. Moreover, he did not want me to change from teaching, which had been his mother's profession and his wife's. A letter dated March 18, 1960, contains further advice on the same theme:

> *I have no doubt you're a good teacher -- every schoolteacher I've ever known periodically doubts his own capacity or liking for the job, especially at this time of the year. Of course that does not mean you have to teach if you prefer something else.*

In reply to something I must have said about marriage, he wrote:

> *It is fun to live with someone one is fond of, it's less lonely, there is more to talk about etc. and of course the sense of intimacy, common interests and adventure, does make life much easier....But don't for heaven's sake marry somebody who is ashamed or prudish about the physical aspect, the body is meant to be enjoyed, and common enjoyment of sex in love is by far the best basis of a happy marriage. It is so much easier to build the other harmonies on that & almost impossible without it -- even though alone it is not enough. But it is a good deal. Even that aspect of marriage of course is much wider than biological needs -- which alone need not worry one much though the need varies of course from one person to another.*

Depression might be helped by marriage, especially a happy one, but most of us have moods of depression, especially reflective people, such as those in our family. “I don't know any remedy except to find something to do which gives one a sense of achievement. I found it at one time in politics, or in writing." People who have one outstanding aim or one great talent have a great advantage over those of us who can do most things well. “I have never had one overwhelming interest and often wondered why in Hades I was doing this or that. It is I think when one finds some interest that really holds one (whether work or hobby) that one is much less given to depression.”

George Grube was a philosopher of the practical school. Plato had inspired him as a refugee boy in his teens to devote his life to the Classics. In 1993, 10 years after his death, George brought in US $22,000 in royalties for translations of his Master. The royalties for 2020 amounted to over US $13,000. That an academic could do that, as well as chairing the founding convention for a new democratic party in Canada, makes him worth remembering.

www.ingramcontent.com/pod-product-compliance
Lightning Source LLC
LaVergne TN
LVHW010948110826
845149LV00015B/3267

* 9 7 8 1 9 8 8 9 2 5 6 7 7 *